Sir Robert Gore Booth and his landed estate in County Sligo, 1814–1876

Maynooth Studies in Local History

SERIES EDITOR Raymond Gillespie

This volume is one of six short books published in the Maynooth Studies in Local History series in 2006. Like their predecessors most are drawn from theses presented as part of the MA course in local history at NUI Maynooth. Also like their predecessors they range widely over the local experience in the Irish past from the middle ages into the twentieth century. That local experience is presented in the complex social world of which it is part. For some this was a case of survival on the margins, whether that be the margins of authority in the medieval pale or the precarious existence of Achill Islanders in the 1930s which forced them to work in Scotland. In other cases the setting was the gentry society built around Castle Caldwell in the eighteenth century. For yet others their world was constructed through the tensions which brought evictions in Luggacurran or the murder of a land-agent in Monaghan. The local experience cannot be a simple chronicling of events relating to an area within administrative or geographically-determined boundaries since understanding the local world presents much more complex challenges for the historian. It is a reconstruction of the socially diverse worlds of poor and rich, for those who owned great estates such as Lisadell and those who emigrated from those estates in search of a better life. Reconstructing such diverse local worlds relies on understanding what the people of the different communities that made up the localities of Ireland had in common and what drove them apart. Understanding the assumptions, often unspoken, around which these local societies operated is the key to recreating the world of the Irish past and reconstructing the way in which those who inhabited those worlds lived their daily lives. As such, studies such as those presented in these short books, together with their predecessors, are at the forefront of Irish historical research and represent some of the most innovative and exciting work being undertaken in Irish history today. They also provide models which others can follow up and adapt in their own studies of the Irish past. In such ways will we understand better the regional diversity of Ireland and the social and cultural basis for that diversity. If they also convey something of the vibrancy and excitement of the world of Irish local history today they will have achieved at least some of their purpose.

Maynooth Studies in Local History: Number 70

Sir Robert Gore Booth and his landed estate in County Sligo, 1814–1876

Land, famine, emigration and politics

Gerard Moran

FOUR COURTS PRESS

Set in 10pt on 12pt Bembo by
Carrigboy Typesetting Services, County Cork for
FOUR COURTS PRESS LTD
7 Malpas Street, Dublin 8, Ireland
e-mail: info@four-courts-press.ie
http://www.four-courts-press.ie
and in North America for
FOUR COURTS PRESS
c/o ISBS, 920 N.E. 58th Avenue, Suite 300, Portland, OR 97213.

10–digit ISBN 1–84682–005–7
13–digit ISBN 978–1–84682–005–2

Printed in Ireland by
ßetaprint, Dublin.

Contents

Acknowledgments

I am indebted for the help and encouragement that I have received from many people during the study and completion of this work. Among those who have been instrumental in this regard have been Dr Tim O'Neill, Dr Patrick Melvin, Dr Brian Dornan, Dr Brian Mac Cuarta, Dr Peter Solar, Professor Tyler Anbinder, Professor Patrick Duffy, Professor Liam Kennedy and Professor Raymond Gillespie. In particular I would like to thank the early groups of students who took the MA in Local History course at NUI Maynooth between 1992 and 1995: inspirational students whose dedication and commitment was a shining example to all who followed. This book is dedicated to the late Jarlath Duffy, one of those students, who exemplified what local history is about: always prepared to share his time, knowledge and expertise of the local history of the west of Ireland. His enthusiasm rubbed off on many people. I would like to thank Deirdre Quinn for permission to reproduce her maps on the Gore Booth estate and Sligo County Library for providing the photograph of Lissadell House. As researchers we would be at a loss without the help and cooperation of the archives and libraries. I am grateful to the Public Record Office of Northern Ireland, Belfast; the National Library of Ireland and the National Archives of Ireland for their assistance and help in locating manuscripts and sources. I am eternally grateful to Eoghan, Cian, Cillian and Caoimhe for their understanding in my love of research and history. To my wife, Clodagh, I am forever in your debt for your love, friendship and support.

Introduction

The Irish landlord in the 19th century has been generally depicted as a ruthless oppressor who cared little for his tenants and lived a life of great opulence and splendour. While there is a certain validity to this image, there has been a partial rehabilitation of the Irish landed proprietor in recent years as research on individual landowners and their estates shows that they were not a homogenous group and in some instances worked hard to improve their properties and the condition of their tenants.[1] Despite this revisionist analysis the Irish landlord remains demonized in folk memory. The landlord had a pivotal influence in the social, economic and political affairs of the area and community that he controlled. Many, such as the earl of Leitrim, ruled their estates with an iron fist, leaving their tenants in no doubt as to their power and authority.[2] Estate rules were implemented that could affect every aspect of the tenants' lives: from who their daughters could marry to the annual whitewashing of their houses. Tenants eligible to vote could be intimidated into voting for the landlord's candidates at election time, the alternative being the threat of eviction from the property. The strongest weapon which the landlord had was the threat of eviction and in a country where there were few alternative employment opportunities to agriculture, this was akin to death.

Many of the Irish landowners were absentees, possessing other estates in the country and in Britain. Their non-residence meant they had little in common with their Irish tenants and in some instances the tenants saw little or nothing of the landlord throughout their lifetimes. The agent represented the landlord on the estate and was the point of contact for the tenants, as he implemented estate policy and was the proprietor's eyes and ears in the locality. This only exacerbated the sense of distance and alienation in the relationship between landlord and tenant.

Sir Robert Gore Booth's estate in Co. Sligo is significant in that he was a resident proprietor who lived locally at Lissadell and controlled 32,000 acres. He also possessed a substantial property in Lancashire in England. While a member of the landed aristocracy and the Church of Ireland, his long reign at Lissadell between 1814 and 1876 was one of estate improvements, looking after his tenants and adopting a paternalistic approach to the people, not only on his property, but among the community at large, during the Great Famine. While Sir Robert has been the subject recently of studies by Deirdre Ryan and Dermot James: the former deals with his role as a landlord during the

Great Famine while the latter looks at him in the context of the family dynasty, they fail to examine the many aspects of his life, as a landowner and and politician. The aim of this work is to examine Gore Booth's involvement in his estates, his relationship with his tenants and the wider community, and his contribution as a political representative at both a national and local level.

A study of an estate such as that of Sir Robert Gore Booth is important for it covers such a large part of the 19th century, and in particular the Great Famine, regarded as a major watershed in Irish history, not only for Irish tenants, but also for Irish landowners. It enables us to examine how a property was managed before the Great Famine, how it coped with the catastrophe of the potato failure and the consequences of the calamity in the immediate decades that followed. The Great Famine resulted in major changes in Irish land ownership as many landowners were forced to sell all or parts of their estates because of the financial difficulties that ensued. The Gore Booth estate is also significant as it allows us to analyze the behaviour of individual Irish landowners who resided on their estates during this period. Contemporary accounts and recent historical analyses indicate that the Irish landed proprietors did little to alleviate the plight of the poor during the Great Famine.[3] Such generalisations treats Irish landlords as a homogenous group and fail to highlight the charitable and philanthropic endeavours of individual landowners to provide relief and assistance during the late 1840s. Some landed proprietors used a variety of methods to help the people: providing food and employment, or in a small number of instances financing and organizing assisted emigration schemes for their tenants to settle in North America.[4] Unfortunately the philanthropic deeds of landowners such as Sir Robert Gore Booth were soon forgotten or ignored in the decades after the Great Famine.

The landlord's power and authority was not just confined to his estate and his tenants, it extended to political control at a local and sometimes at a parliamentary level. Landed proprietors were involved in local politics as poor law guardians, as members of grand juries and as magistrates. Those with large estates tended to serve as the Irish representatives in the house of commons, while others sat in the house of lords. Did they represent their own interests or those of their constituents in these institutions? Up to 1885, when the landlords' dominance of local and national politics finally came to an end, it was often claimed that the proprietors were mainly concerned with looking after the interests of the landed classes and did not represent the views, concerns or problems of all of their constituents, whether they were voters or non-electors. This inevitably led to confrontations and hostility at different stages of the 19th century, especially in the 1850s, 1860s and 1870s. Landlords were in a position to dictate issues at election time through threats and intimidation towards electors, and up to 1885 their opponents failed to organize themselves into a creditable long-term political alternative. It was only with the introduction of the Secret Ballot Act in 1872 and the centralization of popular politics by Charles Stewart Parnell between 1880 and 1885 that the political power of the landlord at a local and parliamentary level came to an end.[5]

Sir Robert Gore Booth and his estate are of importance because we can examine many of these questions: how a large estate in the west of Ireland was managed over a long period in the 19th century, the relationship between landlord and tenant, the role of a landowner during the Great Famine, how the property survived these years of turmoil and the role of the proprietor in local and parliamentary politics. Only through the study of such estates can we evaluate the role of landlords in the 19th century and realize that they were not a uniform group, but that particular circumstances and local experiences moulded their lives and attitudes. Only when other estates are examined will we be able to have a true picture of the Irish landlord and the relationship he had with his tenants and with the wider community.

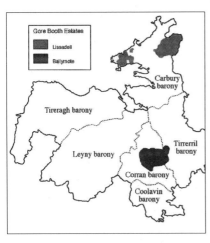

1 The Gore Booth estate in Co. Sligo

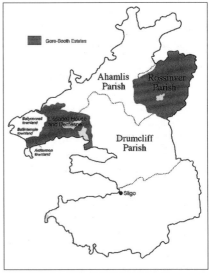

2 The Gore Booth estate in Carbury Barony

1. The Gore Booths and their estate before the Famine

The Gore Booth association with Ireland had its origins with Captain Paul Gore, a soldier of fortune and son of a London alderman, who arrived in Ireland with the earl of Essex in the 1590s, commanding a troop of cavalry. As a result of his military exploits in the Nine Years War and as a reward for capturing Tory Island from the Irish chieftains in 1608, he was granted lands by Elizabeth I and James I, and in 1621 was made a baronet. He built a castle at Ardtermon on the shores of Drumcliff, Co. Sligo, about two miles west of where Sir Robert built his residence, Lissadell House, in 1830. The castle was destroyed by fire in the late 18th century. Over the next 130 years the descendents of Captain Paul Gore acquired lands in Mayo, Leitrim and Donegal, as well as Sligo, and dominated the politics of these counties. In 1711, Sir Paul's great grandson, Nathaniel Gore, married Letitia Booth, the daughter of Humphrey Booth, a Cromwellian settler and from this marriage came the double surname name that the family used.[1] Humphrey Booth had considerable English estates in Manchester and Salford, which came into the possession of the Gore family in 1789 when the last of the Booths died without an heir. The Lancashire estates consisted of Pendlebury, Pendleton, Weaste, Ancoats, Ardwick, Chorlton and Long Millgate. By 1807 the Salford and Manchester properties had an annual rental of £6,240.

Sir Robert Gore Booth was born on 25 August 1805. His father, Sir Robert Newcomen Gore, who took the additional surname and arms of Booth, had succeeded to the estate on the death of his unmarried brother in 1804 and became the third baronet of Lissadell. He was then in his sixties and married almost immediately after taking over the title. His wife, Hannah, was the daughter of Henry Irwin of Streamstown, Co. Sligo. They had two sons and a daughter, Robert, Henry and Anne.[2] Sir Robert was nine when his father died and succeeded to the title in October 1814. He was educated at Westminster College and Queen's College, Cambridge.

In March 1827, Sir Robert married the Hon. Caroline King, daughter of the first Viscount Lorton of Boyle, from Rockingham, Co. Roscommon. As part of the marriage settlement she brought with her a dowry of £10,000. There were other connections with the King family as Sir Robert's sister, Anne, married Caroline's brother, Robert, in December 1829 (he became Viscount Lorton in 1854). However, Caroline died in January 1828, along with her newly born son. In 1830 Gore Booth remarried, to Caroline Susan

Goold, daughter of Thomas Goold of 20 Merrion Square Dublin, and
Dromada, Co. Limerick. She brought a dowry of £2,000.[3] They had two
sons and three daughters. The first son, Robert Newcomen Gore Booth, was
born in 1831, but died in a boating accident in Drumcliff Bay in 1861. His
brother, Henry William, was born in 1843 and took over the estate when his
father died in December 1876. He was father of Constance Gore Booth,
better known as Countess Markievicz.

In 1830 Sir Robert commenced the building of his new residence at
Lissadell, which was completed in 1833. A recent study suggests that Gore
Booth's raison d'etre for building the mansion at Lissadell was to have a
residence that reflected the family's greatly improved circumstances and
position.[4] The original residence at Lissadell suffered flooding during high
tide periods. He chose a site which was several hundred yards inland from
the original house and which had a beautiful view over the bay to the Knock
area. The London architect, Francis Goodwin, who had been involved in the
building of a number of town halls in the Manchester–Salford area, was
employed to draw up the plans. Many of the features for the house came
from ideas that Sir Robert encountered on his travels at home and abroad.
The house's massive geometric shape, in the Greek revival style, reflected the
serious mood of the 1830s and the influence of Gore Booth's extensive
travels in Europe, especially those of Greece and Italy. Architectual features
included an imperial staircase of black Kilkenny marble and a billiard room
to the right of the entrance, used to display the family memorabilia.
Kilkenny marble was also used for the floors. The heart of the house was
dominated by an internal apse-ended room of a cathedral-like scale, 65 feet
long. A large gallery was supported by four great Ionic columns on one side
and engaged Doric piers on the other. A series of sky lights lit the room.
This room was used by Sir Robert as a gallery and music room, with a
Gothic organ, which was built by Hull of Dublin, as the centre piece. It also
had a walnut-topped piano. A bow-ended library which ran from the front
to the back of the house beyond the gallery, had great high windows
allowing natural light to fill the interior. While Lissadell was being built,
Gore Booth embarked on a grand tour of Europe collecting materials and
items for the new residence, including a number of 17th-century Italian
paintings.[5] Access to the domestic offices in the basement was via a sunken
yard and an underground passage which kept the comings and goings of
servants hidden from view. The house was lit by gas[6] and it was the first
major house to have its own gas supply, which was produced by a plant that
Sir Robert had built about a quarter of a mile from Lissadell. The house could
be approached from three routes and was one of the last great neo-classical
houses built in Ireland. There were many similarities with Rockingham, Co.
Roscommon, the residence of Sir Robert's first father-in-law, Lord Lorton.

Sir Robert's original intention was to cap the building cost at £10,000. Goodwin's first proposal was £4,500 over budget, but eventually the expenditure was fixed at £11,701. Goodwin and the contractor, James Nowell, were forced to make many adjustments and reductions: costs were controlled by using local grey limestone from Ballysadare throughout the building.[7] Money was also spent on the demesne with 120 acres being planted with trees between 1832 and 1833. A large walled garden, which covered two acres, was also created which provided Lissadell with most of its vegetables and fruit. Local labour was employed in all of the work. The house and demesne suffered badly on 'The Night of the Big Wind', on 6 January 1839. Thousands of trees were damaged or lost, including many exotic species which Sir Robert had introduced, a number of valuable cattle killed and nearly all of the outhouses reduced to ruins.[8] All were replaced or repaired.

Lissadell quickly became an important centre for the social life of the landed gentry in north Sligo. However, the building did have its problems. According to one frequent guest at Lissadell, the kitchen was full of rats who came in and out of a hole in the ground. Visitors played a game to see how many rats could be killed.[9] Between 20 and 26 June 1846, 109 rats were killed in the kitchen, 101 in the stockyard, 60 in the hen house and 39 in the cow house. Smoking was forbidden in the house, because of Sir Robert's aversion to it, so unlike the houses of most other landed gentry, no smoking room was provided. Sir Robert believed that smoking was only 'fit for servants and grooms' and any gentleman who wished to do so had to go the kitchens. This led some visitors to form the Pig and Whistle Club in the kitchen.[10]

One of Gore Booth's great passions was hunting. Stables were built on the demnese, which also had a riding school, and a pack of hunting hounds was kept. The Lissadell hunt was one of the social highlights in the north Sligo area. Lissadell also became a centre for entertainment and socializing, with many of the local gentry and visitors to north Sligo staying there. Among the regulars who came to dinner were the Wynnes, the Parkers, the Jefficots, the Irwins, the Coopers, the Palmerstons and the Enniskillens. When he was not at Lissadell, Gore Booth spent much of his time sailing, going to the Outer Hebrides and the Mediterranean. Yachting was a great passion and for three to four months each year he set off on boating trips around Britain and Ireland. He was also an active fisherman and spent much time fishing on the nearby rivers and lakes.

Sir Robert was exceptional among the larger landowners of Co. Sligo in that he resided on his Irish estate. He lived at Lissadell throughout the years 1830 to 1848 except for a three-year period and was well acquainted with local conditions and needs, unlike other proprietors, such as Lord Palmerston, who only visited his Sligo estate periodically. Residency had important consequences for the landlord's local political power and for the local economy.

As Sir Robert was based at Lissadell for most of the year, a considerable portion of his rents, not only from Sligo but also from Lancashire, were spent locally. Servants and domestics were employed at Lissadell, stable boys looked after his horses, and locals were paid to look after the hounds. In 1840, Mr L'Antoine, the French cook, received £84 in wages; the coachman, Mr Carew, got £31 10s., J. Fogate, the footman, earned £25 4s., and James Stewart, the house stewart, £63.[11] Labourers were employed on the demesne earning 8d. a day. Local artisans and craftsmen were brought in to supply the needs of the house and the family. Accounts were kept with local shopkeepers and merchants such as Richard Smith, Grocer, Wine and Spirit Merchant of 10 Knox Street, Sligo, and with Leech and Sons of Sligo. In contrast, absentee landlords spent much of their Irish rents in London, Bath and other English cities.[12] Their local political interests could not always be looked after by their agents. The significance of Sir Robert's residency can be noted in the role he played with the Sligo board of guardians and the other local bodies that he was involved with. Sir Robert seems to have taken to heart the advice he received at age 15 from Andrew Motherwell in July 1820. Motherwell claimed that the country suffered when landlords lived outside of Ireland and if they spent more time on their properties it would help contain rebellions and encourage their tenants to be more industrious.[13] Sir Robert's residency was also praised by Sir Henry Coulter, who visited the estate in the early 1860s, and stated that if other landowners resided on their properties 'the cry of distress which is so often raised … would never more be raised, even in the west of Ireland'.[14]

While Gore Booth resided at Lissadell, the day-to-day running of the property was left to an agent, George Dowdell, who lived in Sligo town and managed a large number of estates in the county. He was appointed agent in November 1823 and given power of attorney over the estate.[15] As the property was scattered it was important that an agent managed the estate. This does not mean that Sir Robert did not retain a major involvement. He had a good relationship with Dodwell, as is indicated from the agent's evidence before the Devon commission and in the estate's correspondence. While agents made important contributions to the running of properties it was the resolve and character of the landowner that decided and controlled estate policy. While agents could institute change, the landlord ensured continuity. However, in the case of the Gore Booth estate, both Dodwell and the proprietor played important roles in the management and development of the property. One of Dodwell's first acts on taking up the position was to actively discourage rundale. According to Francis Barber, prior to the agent's appointment the people lived in small squalid cabins that were part of a clachan system. They spent much of their time quarrelling and fighting over their strips of land, were in arrears with their rents, and the estate was uneconomical. Dodwell squared the farms and stipulated that each tenant built his own little house on his farm.[16] Some indication of his remuneration is suggested from the estate papers. For the period 1833–7 he received £1,302 10s. for the agency of the Ballymote property and in 1840 got £289 3s. 3d. for the Lissadell lands.[17] In September 1843 he retired and was replaced by Richard Getting.

The Gore Booth property of Lissadell was in the Sligo poor law union and comprised fifty-three townlands in the electoral divisions of Carney, Lissadell and Rossiver. They were in the religious parishes of Drumcliff and Rossiver, with one townland in the parish of Ahamlish. In 1810 the property, which comprised 12,000 statute acres, had an annual rental of £3,300 and a valuation of £7,720. There were 48 principal tenants, all had leases of up to three lives.[18] The combined poor law valuation for the three electoral divisions was £11,655.[19]

As with most other parts of pre-Famine Ireland Co. Sligo was heavily populated and congested. In 1821 the population was 146,229 and this increased to 171,508 in 1831 and 180,882 in 1841. At the time of the Great Famine it had a population density of more than 300 per square mile and in some places it was over 400. The electoral divisions of Carney, Lissadell and Rossiver in north Sligo had a combined population in the 1840s of 12,509 with Lissadell being the most populous with 6,420 people. Between 1821 and 1841 the population of the barony of Carbury increased from 40,518 to 46,597. There was a very high demand for tenancies. By 1836 the average size of farm in the barony was three acres and cottiers paid about £2 to a middle man for a cabin with one-half to one acre of land.[20] The problem of over-population was most acute in the parish of Drumcliff. The townland of Ballyconnell had 143 families with 719 individuals living on 1,018 acres, 578 of which were regarded as agriculturally poor. Rents ranged from 15s. to 30s. an acre. There were 79 families, 349 people, living on 315 acres at Carrigeens and 50 acres were said to be worthless. Forty-five families, comprising 260 people lived on 307 acres on the townland of Mount Edward and 257 acres were considered to be marginal or bad. The total rental for the townland was £22 18s. 4d. The thirty-eight families living on Clooneely were heavily in arrears and unable to pay their rents because of the poor quality of the land.[21] Ardtarmon covered 145 acres, but only 45 acres were arable, the rest consisting of sand dunes, marsh and water. Prior to 1847 there were 31 families, comprising between 185 and 200 individuals, living in the townland which had an annual rent of £102 13s 2d. They struggled to survive and by March 1847 owed £1,130 5s. 4d. in rent arrears. Between 1840 and 1847 only two tenants had paid all of their rent, the rest paying nothing.[22]

Other environmental factors made it difficult survive on the land. Near the coast, particularly in the townlands of Ardtarmon, Raghly and Ballyconnell, some lands were unusable because of sand drifting from the seashore. In 1838 it was feared that the problem would extend to other parts of the estate. Although initially Sir Robert had difficulty persuading neighbouring proprietors, such as Lord Palmerston, whose estate was ten miles north of Lissadell, to participate in joint action to improve these lands, by the 1840s both Palmerston and Gore Booth were planting bent near the seashore to prevent sand drifting onto the adjoining cultivated lands.[23]

Sir Robert addressed the House of Lords Select Committee on Colonisation from Ireland in 1847 stating that in north Sligo the majority of the tenants would not be able to exist even if they paid no rent, rates or taxes of any kind.[24] Yet Gore Booth charged from 25s. to 30s. an acre in rent for his lands in Carbury barony in the 1840s, and tenants on the Palmerston estate were expected to pay 20s. to 30s. an acre. The population existed on potatoes and, being close to the coast, used sea weed as manure to produce high yields.[25] Those who lived close to the coast supplemented their diet with fish.

Congestion and over-population was not just a problem on the Gore Booth property: it was rampant on neighbouring estates such as at that of Lord Palmerston. Congestion and poverty were largely associated with the middleman system where leases were given to tenants who then sublet the lands resulting in small unviable holdings. Rundale was also related to the middleman system where tenants received strips of land in a number of areas. As leases were for up to 31 years Sir Robert and other proprietors could make few changes until the lease ended. Most landowners wanted to improve their estates and consolidate the holdings and opposed the middleman system, not because of the impact it had on the sub-tenants, but because they believed that they should be getting the money that came from rents.[26] Middlemen also tended to be more severe on their tenants than the landlords might have been.[27] On many estates middlemen facilitated the subdivision of plots, much to the anger of the proprietors. This had been prevalent in the north Sligo area at the end of the 18th century and during the Napoleonic wars. At Mullaghmore on the Palmerston estate, 135 tenants lived on 201 Irish acres, but only 50 paid their rent directly to the landlord, the rest paying to middlemen.[28] Most landowners and agents maintained that it was difficult to stamp out subdivision, even when the estate rules prohibited the practice. The mistakes, errors and lack of planning of earlier generations allowed the problem of poverty, fragmentation and rent arrears to fester. These issues had to be tackled and addressed as a matter of urgency in the 1830s and 1840s.[29]

A common question before the Great Famine was the minimum size of holding needed to support a family. This obviously depended on the fertility of the land. According to the land agent, William Sherrard, a witness before the Devon commission, the minimum needed in Connacht was from six to eight acres, while Sir Robert felt that no holding should be less than four acres.[30] He argued that a twenty-five acre farm would maintain a family in comfort, but this could only be achieved by removing the surplus population from the overpopulated regions.[31] When the Great Famine occurred the farm-size on the Lissadell estate ranged from one to 25 acres with the average being 10 to 12 acres.[32] Just 12 per cent of the Gore Booth holdings in the parish of Drumcliff were under 5 acres, while 53 per cent were between five and 15 acres.[33]

Gore Booth was one of the first landowners in pre-Famine Ireland to examine the question of poverty and congestion in Ireland and to suggest possible remedies. As early as 1823, at the age of eighteen, he concluded that radical changes were needed to avoid a major catastrophe. Consolidation of holdings into viable units was vital. Later in 1847 he stated: 'I have at all times endeavoured to increase the size of the farms and in a manner that was consistent with justice to the individual.'[34] As the Lissadell estate was scattered over three parishes it was difficult to implement uniform change. As a result Sir Robert concentrated his efforts on the Drumcliff portion, introducing new rules, regulations and improvements. This was the best policy to adopt as limited resources meant funding was not available for the entire estate. In the 1830s he built a harbour at Raughly, which was designed by Alexander Nimmo, to improve fishing in the area.[35] A concerted attempt was made to eliminate rundale. As leases fell in, the land was divided among the small holders and, where insufficient land was available, the tenants were offered farms on other parts of the estate which could accommodate them. When land was not available the tenants received compensation for their houses and for any improvements they had carried out and were given the passage fare to North America. This first occurred in 1834 when Mr Martin's lease ended: this middleman held 800 acres at Ballygilgan near Lissadell. The townland contained a large number of sub-tenants holding less than four acres, many of whom were unable to exist on the land.[36] Eighteen tenants refused to accept the passage fare to North America and were given holdings in Lissadell, Cloonmullen, Ballintemple, Cartonwilliamoge, Cooladrumman, Cillaghmore and Ballygilgin itself.[37] The changes at Ballygilgan cost Sir Robert £3,788 18s. 3d., including the cost of pulling down houses, land improvements, passage costs to North America in 1839 and 1841, and wages for constructing roads, leveling ditches and other work on the estate.[38] Yet, subdivision remained a major problem in north Sligo up to the Great Famine. Even after the Famine a number of townlands, such as Carrigeens remained congested and overpopulated, and Sir Robert continued to consolidate holdings up to the 1870s.[39]

This does not imply that Sir Robert opposed the granting of leases in specific circumstances. In particular, he granted them to tenants who improved their farms. One such case was Francis Barber who lived at Rahelly, near Carney and started off in the 1820s with a 20-acre farm. In 1840 he received a ninety-acre farm at Rahelly with a lease for two lives and in 1844 was given a 160-acre farm at Cooladruma, 48 acres of which was under tillage. He spent £1,300 of his own in draining, reclaiming and manuring these lands which became some of the most profitable lands at Lissadell. This initiative earned him additional land and a reduction in rent from 31s. to 24s. 9d. an acre. The landlord was so impressed that Barber received a lease for three lives at Gorteen in 1851. When Sir Robert died in 1876 Francis Barber was the largest tenant on the estate, farming over 450 acres.[40] It was estimated that he had improved the value of the land from 5s. to 30s. per acre. By 1861 he had put down 2,600 perches in drains and 150 acres of land was under tillage and meadow, the rest – marginal land – was used for grazing. He had 160 head of cattle and a large stud of horses. Local people were employed on his lands and his annual wage bill came to £1,100.[41]

In the decades prior to the Famine, Gore Booth and other landowners in north Sligo attempted to implement agricultural improvements on their estates. On the neighbouring Palmerston property the landlord offered premiums for improvements, seeds were given on credit to the tenants every year and £30 a year was distributed among the small farmers for green crops to encourage crop rotation. £15,000 was also provided to improve Mullaghmore harbour and thus encourage the fishing industry.[42] Sir Robert was also regarded as a good, improving landlord who tried to better the lives and conditions of his tenants. Between 1834 and 1842 £4,000 was spent on improvements and tenants were also employed on the demesne.[43] Tenants were encouraged and assisted to drain their lands, and slates were provided for buildings and timber for the roofs, doors, door cases and windows of new houses. A plan was provided for each house. One rule, which was strictly enforced, ensured that all tenants whitewashed their homes before 1 April each year. George Dodwell, the agent, or his representatives visited each house to enforce this instruction. This put an additional burden on the tenants as it had to be carried out at a time of year when they were busy with spring sowing and was often undertaken during bad weather.[44] While the tenants felt the landlord was dictatorial in enforcing this rule, it was done for hygiene reasons. The new rules had a positive impact and Perton Hart reported that he came across many comfortable cottages around Lissadell. Lady Gore Booth offered a premium of a cow for the best kept cabin on the estate.[45] Money was also made available to improve the road system within the estate and by 1833 68 miles of new roads had been built under Dodwell's supervision.[46]

Sir Robert was convinced that the reclamation of wastelands was an unprofitable exercise. During the 1830s he had tried to improve the marginal lands, but felt it brought little benefit to the people's living standards.[47] He believed that while tenants could be encouraged to improve their agricultural skills and methods, as long as the holdings remained small the land would not support them. Even a three-acre farm with good land was unlikely to be adequate to sustain a family.[48] He consequently discontinued the practice of reclaiming waste lands and diverted the money towards helping the tenants to emigrate. Improvements were financed by a loan fund where tenants borrowed money at a favourable rate. In 1833 Gore Booth's father-in-law, Thomas Goold, suggested that a sinking fund be established to pay for such improvements: £4,000 was made available for Lissadell, £6,500 for Ballymote and £3,000 for the Lancashire properties.[49]

In the early 1830s Sir Robert took the unusual step of building up his Irish property portfolio, using the Manchester and Salford estates to finance the purchase of lands in Ballymote, Co. Sligo. This was at a time when property prices and rentals in Lancashire were increasing because of the Industrial Revolution. At the same time returns from Irish property were uncertain because of crop failures and the depression in agricultural prices in the post Napoleonic war period, making it a good time to buy Irish land. Gore Booth was showing a commitment and confidence in the Irish land market which was exceptional as many of his peers were uncertain about the long-term viability and returns from Irish property. A long-standing mortgage of £12,000 on the Lissadell estate was paid off in 1828 and in the early 1830s he invested heavily in buying new property in Co. Sligo. In August 1833 he bought the Ballymote estate of the Fitzmaurice family, the earls of Orkney, for £130,000. The 16,000 acre property comprised 64 townlands and included part of Ballymote town. The purchase was financed in a number of ways: a £20,000 mortgage was secured on the strength of the Manchester and Salford properties and another £79,000 was raised through selling the rents of some of the English properties.[50] While the purchase of the Ballymote lands trebled the rents from the Sligo properties, there was a noticeable income reduction from the Lancashire estates: from £6,240 in 1807 to £2,140 in 1834 and £2,868 in 1880.[51]

While the financial rationale for concentrating on the Irish property market may be questioned, the purchase did have merits. Gore Booth became one of the largest landowners in Co. Sligo with 32,500 acres and this raised his political and social status and profile in the county. He was now a major political power broker for the county's parliamentary seats because of the large number of voters on his estates. No aspiring politician could ignore his patronage. This position of influence can be seen at the 1848 general election when Charles Townley, who was seeking a nomination in Sligo, wrote a letter of introduction to Sir Robert in the hope that he would publicly support him.[52] There were occasions when Gore Booth himself was mentioned as a possible parliamentary candidate, most notably in 1847. It was not until 1850 that he allowed his name to go forward as a Conservative candidate. Even more significant was his status within Sligo: he was governor of the Sligo and Leitrim Hospital for the Insane; a governor of the Sligo

County Infirmary, vice-chairman of Sligo Board of Guardians and a member of the board of superintendence for Sligo County Prison. In 1830 he became the sheriff of Sligo, in 1841 deputy lieutenant of the county. On 7 December 1868 he became lord lieutenant of Sligo, a position he held until his death in December 1876.

While great efforts were made to improve the estate and the tenants' position, a constant difficulty up to the 1840s was the collection of rents. The problem with rent arrears dated back to his father's time. By 1820 many tenants on the Lissadell estate were slow in making their payments, with the agricultural crisis brought about by ending of the Napoleonic war making it difficult to bring in outsiders who could pay the rent. Andrew Motherwell told Gore Booth in July 1820 'if any of them are dispossessed for non-payment of rent, the holding will be waste for perhaps upwards of a year – the whole order of tenantry being in combination with each other against the landlords that no one will take or interfere with any holding that a tenant is turned out of, or will strangers come in to the country or take or offer a shilling for lands …'.[53] In 1837 of the 310 tenants on Ballymote property who paid rents directly to Sir Robert 86 owed £1,689 15s. 9d., 51 owed over £5 with John Gorman of Clooshanbally owing £83 1s. 6d. and William Alexander of Brickview owing £69 19s. 4d.[54] This was a prelude to the problems that all landlords faced during the Famine years. In 1843 the annual rents for the Lissadell property amounted to £4,581, but a total of £5,796 was outstanding in rent arrears with the Ballymote portion of the estate continuing to be unsatisfactory.[55] While all sections of the Lissadell estate had problems with rent payments, those with holdings over 50 acres were largely solvent. A total of 51 per cent of those with farms under 5 acres owed more than one year's rent, while 16 per cent in the 5 to 15 acres category were in arrears.[56]

While Sir Robert had a good relationship with his tenants there were occasions when tensions arose. In 1838 he was accused of evicting a number of his tenants for having voted for Mr Somers in the general election and for having refused to support his nominee.[57] It was claimed that they were given £2 each by Gore Booth and sent to North America. Sir Robert strenuously denied the accusation that their removal was connected with the election, arguing that it was associated with the consolidation of holdings. It was also alleged that the tenants had been sent to North America on the *Pompona*, an unseaworthy vessel, and that a number had drowned. The allegation was totally unfounded, but the myth remained until recent times. Recent research indicates the *Pompona* continued to operate as a merchant vessel for many years afterwards.[58] There was also trouble on the estate as illegal agrarian organizations carried out attacks on property and people. In September 1842 two tenants from the estate, believed to be Ribbonmen, were arrested as they were in the process of carrying out illegal activities.[59]

An unspecified outrage, committed on Sir Robert's property in October 1845, led the tenants of Carney to organize a meeting, which was chaired by the local parish priest, Fr Patrick O'Gara, to condemn the attack. A fund was established for information leading to the conviction of the perpetrators, intimated to be outsiders. The tenants expressed their total allegiance to Sir Robert and stated he had improved their lives and that he allowed them 'the fullest liberty of conscience, whether political or religious'.[60]

2. Sir Robert Gore Booth and the Great Famine in north Sligo

By the early 1840s three million people in Ireland, over 40 per cent of the total population, were totally dependent on the potato as their main source of food. As 45 per cent of Irish holdings were under five acres the potato increasingly became the mainstay of the people. The situation in Co. Sligo was more acute as 61 per cent of the farms were under five acres, or as Sir Robert Gore Booth had maintained, unviable. As a result the population of Sligo was heavily dependent on the potato for survival, despite the fact that some landowners such as Gore Booth and Lord Palmerston had attempted to consolidate the holdings and implement improvements on their estates. Tenants on these small holdings enjoyed a reasonable subsistence existence while the potato crop was plentiful, but the threat of a calamity was never far off if the potato failed. Many, including Gore Booth, prophesied an imminent catastrophe because of this over-reliance, and were proved right when the potato crop failed in the autumn of 1845.

In 1845 the potato crop partially failed, but the crisis was not as bad in north Sligo as elsewhere in the country. In September there was no indication that the potato was in danger. The constabulary report from Ballymote on 22 September stated that the potato had the appearance of being plentiful, a better crop than for many years.[1] The earliest report of the crop's failure occurred on 10 October when it was stated that the rot had appeared near Sligo town; near Ballymote the blight was extensive and 'potatoes which appeared sound when digging, rotted shortly afterwards'.[2] However, people were not alarmed, probably because of previous crises with the potato crop in the decades prior to 1845, as in 1822 when it was estimated that about 50 per cent of the population of the country needed relief because of the potato failure.[3] In December 1845 it was stated that many people would have no potatoes by the following April, but no major concern was expressed. Gore Booth told the Sligo board of guardians in December that all of the potatoes around Lissadell were eaten, but that towards the coast at Cliffony and Rossinver most of the crop was still good.[4] In Drumcliff, half of the potatoes were rotten.[5] By the spring of 1846 great want was being reported from Sligo. In April a large group of labourers walked to the Sligo board of guardians meeting and begged for assistance.[6]

While one-third of the crop was lost in 1845, the situation was a catastrophe in 1846 when three quarters of the potatoes were blighted. The yield in Sligo declined from 8.3 tons per acre in 1845 to less than half a ton the following year.[7] The problem was largely due to the eleven inches of rain that fell in June, July and August, compared to an average of six to seven inches for the summer months.[8] No area of the county was spared from the ravages of blight. By mid-July the first reports of the devastation appeared and by late October it was clear that the crop was severely damaged: one half of the stalks were withered and the potatoes small and tainted. The hopes of the poor were destroyed after the problems with the previous year's crop and 'unless God averts the evil, they have now before them another year of want and suffering, disease and misery'. This observer noted further that the unpredictability of the potato was such that an alternative food supply needed to be introduced.[9] The crop in Ballymote was totally lost and the 'multitudes are in utter destitution … Actual starvation will visit and lay waste many of the most populous villages in the district', and it would lead to lawlessness as the people sought food to keep their families alive.[10] Reports from the Palmerston estate in August 1846 stated that the potato crop was a total failure and 200 families were destitute. By November there were 1,500 distressed families, numbering 9,700 people, in Ahamlish.[11] Alternative food supplies were quickly exhausted and by November 1846 no meal was available in Ballymote. This prompted the local Church of Ireland rector, the Revd John Garrett, to complain that the poor people were being left to the mercy of hucksters who charged enormous prices.[12]

The government's response in 1845 and 1846 was in the main modest and not adequate to counteract the crisis. In November 1845, the prime minister, Sir Robert Peel, ordered the secret purchase of £100,000 worth of Indian corn in North America and this was sent to depots around the country and then distributed. The purpose of the exercise was not to feed the people, but to keep the market price of corn down and within the reach of the poor. The main distribution depot in the north-west was Sligo town; it was in operation between July and August 1846. The other government measure was the establishment of public works in early 1846, which were controlled by the Board of Works and not by the grand juries. All charges would be financed by local taxation. By December 1846, 441,000 people were employed on the works and it peaked in March 1847 with 714,390 persons. The relief works were very bureaucratic and there were problems with the payments to the workers. In October 1846, the Revd John Garrett of the Corran Relief Committee reported the death of an able-bodied labourer who was earning 8*d.* a day on the works but who had not been paid for ten days. He and his family had survived on cabbage for the previous four days and at his death he left a widow with six children.[13]

The government never regarded itself as being the principal vehicle for the provision of relief during the Famine. Its attitude was that Irish land should pay for the maintenance of the poor and for relief. Landlords such as

Sir Robert Gore Booth were expected to take responsibility for the financing of such relief: it was a responsibility that the majority of proprietors could not and would not undertake. Gore Booth was an exception.

Sir Robert's role in aiding the people of north Sligo during the Great Famine has been largely unacknowledged by historians, principally because he did not seek publicity for his philanthropy in helping the population of Lissadell and Ballymote. His involvement was confined to four areas: as a member of the Sligo board of guardians, as chairman of the Sligo grand jury, as chairman of four local relief committees, and through the private relief measures he initiated around his properties.

Sligo workhouse opened in December 1841 with accommodation for 1,200 inmates. The government wanted the poor law to be at the forefront of the relief operations during the Famine, but the unions were unable to cope with the demands that a famine situation placed on them. Sir George Nichols, the architect of the Irish poor law when it was established in 1838, informed the government when the system was first introduced, that it would be unable to deal with a major famine. By the autumn of 1846 most of the workhouses along the western seaboard were struggling to cope with the pressures of inmate numbers and declining income. In the early stages the unions were only allowed to provide aid within the confines of the workhouses and there was no provision for outdoor relief. By November 1846 the Sligo workhouse was full, as large numbers of labourers were admitted because the 8*d.* a day they received on the public works could not support them and their families. £13,000 was owed to contractors and the guardians applied unsuccessfully to the government for a £3,000 loan. The union was informed it would have to rely on its own resources. In an attempt to cut costs the guardians, with Gore Booth present, decided to reduce the amount of food that the inmates received and a soup kitchen was set up for the poor offering soup at 1*d.* per portion.[14]

Gore Booth became a guardian for Lissadell when the board of guardians for Sligo was established in 1841. He resigned his seat in order to get an additional guardian for the division and became an ex-officio member of the board. By 1845 he was deputy chairman of the board.[15] Between 1845 and 1850 he was not a regular attender at the weekly board meetings, but this can be attributed to the amount of time that he spent with the four local relief committees and his belief that the poor law guardians were not in a position to save the people. Non-attendance by the guardians was a major problem with the Sligo Union and the Dublin authorities issued a circular in December 1847 calling on the proprietors to help with the relief oper-ations.[16] Despite his absences Gore Booth continued to perform important functions for the union. In March 1847 the lord lieutenant appointed him chairman of the Relief Finance Committee for Sligo Union and it was responsible for ordering relief materials during 1847. It was generally acknowledged that Gore Booth carried out these tasks very efficiently.[17] This was at a time when the union was facing enormous difficulties: by July 1847, 48 per cent of the population in the union were being given relief with 53 per cent of Rossinver and 24 per cent in Carney on the lists.[18] The crisis in the union was so great that no new inmates were being admitted to the workhouse. On 26 October 1847 between 200 and 300 destitute persons assembled outside the workhouse gate and unsuccessfully pleaded to be admitted or given employment.[19] The pressure increased and by 1847, 130 old and infirm inmates and their children were discharged and replaced by 250 able-bodied paupers. The workhouse was grossly overcrowded, but many destitute people could not gain admission.[20] While the number of inmates continued to rise – by the end of November 1848 there were 2,437 inmate paupers – the union was unable to collect the rates to finance the administration of the poor law. The union was on the verge of bankruptcy on a number of occasions, as in October 1847. Many proprietors were unable to pay their rates because of their tenants' inability to pay the rent or because tenants had emigrated without paying their rents. The marquis of Sligo, who had an extensive estate in Co. Mayo, received no rents between 1845 and 1848 and the problem was greatest where a large proportion of the farms were small, with valuations under £4.[21] In the Lissadell electoral division there were 787 occupiers of land of whom 63 per cent were rated at under £4. The average size of holding was 2.75 acres. Those with property over the £4 valuation had an average of only 9.6 acres. Carney electoral division had 715 occupiers of land and 52 per cent were rated at under £4 and had holdings with an average of 2.8 acres. Those with farms over the £4 valuation held properties with an average size of 24 acres. In the Rossinver electoral division, 30 per cent of the 317 occupiers were under the £4 valuation, with the remainder holding farms which averaged 24 acres, but much of this was poor mountainous land.[22]

On 23 December 1846 a meeting of landed proprietors, including Gore Booth, and cesspayers took place in Sligo and resolutions were passed stating that taxation for the relief of the poor should not place a heavy burden on landlords.[23] While proprietors such as Sir Robert had greatly improved their estates prior to the Famine they had to finance those landlords who had not taken care of their properties. The administrative unit for the collection of the poor law was the electoral division.[24] Four other proprietors owned lands in the electoral divisions of Lissadell, Carney and Rossinver – Sir Gilbert King, Captain Michael Kelly, Charles Gore Jones and John Gethin – and distress was greatest on these estates. In effect Sir Robert was subsidizing them for he had to pay towards the upkeep of all of the poor in these electoral divisions. In 1843 the poor rate in Lissadell was 5*d.* in the £, but by June 1847 this had increased to 6*s.* 8*d.* in the £. As James Hack Tuke, who reported from the west of Ireland for the Society of Friends in 1847, said, 'if each proprietor was responsible only for the rates on his own land, he would in many cases, soon free himself from the burden of pauperism by the profitable employment of the labourers on his estate'.[25] Gore Booth hoped for a more equitable situation and that the arrears of poor rates be collected. In 1848 he offered to provide and furnish accommodation in Ballymote for the military so that the poor rate collectors could be protected as they collected the rate arrears.[26]

As chairman of the Sligo grand jury, greater benevolence in the provision of public works schemes might have been expected of Gore Booth. In the early stages of the Famine he displayed a reluctance to sanction works as with the proposal to build a road from Sligo to Raghly, arguing that it was not feasible until the congested population was removed from the affected townlands. As a result of this reluctance to sanction works only 9,285 people were employed on the relief works in Sligo on 1 August 1846 and 2,584 were employed in the barony of Carbury.[27] By December, 2,208 people were working on the relief works in Corran barony of whom 357 were women.[28] There was a major need for these works, and at the extraordinary special sessions for the barony of Carbury on 14 December 1846 it was stated that £11,000 was required to support the people of Ahamlish for three months, but the poor law valuation for the division was only £3,000; 8,000 out of a population of 10,000 were totally destitute.[29] As the ravages of the Famine became more devastating Gore Booth became more convinced of the need for public works. In late February 1847 he chaired the extraordinary presentment sessions for the barony of Carbury at the Sligo Courthouse. Despite the opposition of many local landowners a total of £30,000 was passed for works and a large sum allocated to Ahamlish.[30]

Gore Booth's contribution and commitment to the relief operations in north Sligo can be noted in that he was chairman of four relief committees that bordered Lissadell: Carney, Rossinver, Drumcliff and Lissadell. Although not a member of the Corran relief committee, which took in the Ballymote portion of his property (probably because of the distance from his residence at Lissadell), he forwarded a financial contribution of £100.[31] Of greater importance was Sir Robert's decision to provide direct assistance to the people on his Ballymote property. This allowed the Corran Relief Committee to concentrate its operations on the remaining destitute population.[32] This was probably a better arrangement as there was acrimony between the different groups on the committee: the Church of Ireland rector, John Garrett, was in dispute with the local Catholic clergy alleging that the priests were placing some of their parishioners on the relief lists, not because they were destitute but because they had provided large contributions for the upkeep of the priests.[33]

The first of the local relief committees on the Gore Booth estate was established in Drumcliff in June 1846, mainly at Sir Robert's behest. It was primarily concerned with the plight of the cottiers and very small farmers who during years of plenty had difficulty providing for their families during the hungry months. The Carney Relief Committee was founded in August 1846 and the Lissadell committee around the same time. The Lissadell committee included the two local Catholic priests, one being Fr Patrick O'Gara, together with the local Church of Ireland rector, the Revd William Jeffcott. In February 1847 Gore Booth provided each of the four relief committees with a £150 donation.

The four local relief committees concentrated much of their efforts on the setting up of soup kitchens, mainly due to Sir Robert's urgings. The establishment of soup kitchens has been generally regarded as one of the more beneficial aspects of the Famine relief operations. They were first introduced in Cork city in November 1846 by the Society of Friends and were regarded as a cheap and effective way of feeding the people. A major advantage was that soup greatly reduced the incidence of diarrhoea and dysentery, the main killers of people during the Famine, and which had been prevalent with the Indian corn that had initially been used in the relief operations. In February 1847 the soup kitchens became the main government relief measure after the public works program was reduced. In May 1847 the Lissadell Relief Committee purchased boilers to make soup for the people in Ballinfull, Cloghwhisky, Rockley, Ballyconnell, Ardtarmon and Breaghwy.[34] A similar approach was adopted by the Corran Relief Committee where five soup kitchens were opened in May 1847 and 4,000 of the most destitute people fed daily.[35]

Gore Booth's commitment to these operations can be noted in that he attended 70 per cent of the meetings of the four relief committees between 1846 and 1850. Such obligations took up much of his time. One day each week there were meetings in Sligo which lasted from 10 o'clock in the morning till 7 o'clock in the evening. His involvement with the four local committees took up two to three days each week.[36] These exertions eventually affected his health and in the summer of 1847 he contracted famine fever. His role was taken over by his wife, Lady Caroline, who worked from eleven in the morning till late at night distributing food, often in constant rain and intense cold.[37]

Gore Booth put most of his efforts into the alleviation of distress round his Lissadell estate. As early as November 1845 he set up a mill at Lissadell to grind diseased potatoes and in January 1846 he returned £150 of conacre rents according to the losses sustained by the occupiers. He also increased the number of labourers employed at Lissadell.[38] During August 1846 he paid out a total of £1,721 to local merchants for food to be distributed amongst the destitute population and in 1847 a further £13,403 was spent on relief, mainly food that was purchased abroad and brought in through Sligo port.[39] Two soup boilers were purchased which distributed 28 gallons of soup each day to the poor of Lissadell at a cost of 65s. One hundred and fifty loaves of bread were sold each day at the cost price of 2*d*. and thirty tons of Indian meal were given to those tenants who could not afford to pay. Between the end of August and early December 1847 Sir Robert distributed 393 tons of Indian meal, 70 tons of flour, 40 tons of whole meal flour and nine tons of biscuits. The crew of his yacht were employed as cooks and bakers, and all of the Lissadell household were engaged in the relief effort.[40] In addition he paid for twenty-four coffins in January-February so that people could be buried. Some people were being buried at night and without any religious ceremonies because their relatives could not afford a coffin.[41]

By the spring of 1847 Gore Booth was convinced that the government's public relief works was doing little for the starving population. By January there was extreme want around Lissadell. There were twenty stacks of oats amongst the 2,000 individuals in Ballyconnell townland and virtually all of the population in north Sligo were described as destitute. In March 1847, Captain O'Brien of the Board of Works reported great destitution in the region and wrote of one house that 'The children were bloated in their faces and bodies, their limbs withered to bones and sinews, with rags on them which scarcely preserved decency, and assuredly afforded no protection from the weather.'[42] The problem for the people was twofold: most had consumed their seed potatoes and they had nothing to plant, and no relief was available. Sir Robert was informed that the destitution was so great the people were dying, but they accepted the situation as normal. On 6 February 1847, Mr Halliday, the inspecting officer for Co. Sligo, stated: 'The people are quiet, suffering, but most apathetic'.[43] Every article of clothes and furniture had been sold in order to purchase food and now nothing remained. The public works were unable to give adequate aid and many of the local landowners were unable or unwilling to give assistance. Sir Robert was asked to try and secure a £50,000 government grant for the impoverished districts, for 'the landlords of this district are unable to assert themselves, or repay any money advanced'.[44] Sir Robert saw little point in making overtures to the government and it was about this time that he purchased boilers to provide soup for the poor.

The problems which the Lissadell estate encountered during the Famine years were exacerbated by a number of factors: the location of the property in a county that was severely hit by the potato failure, the high number of small holdings on the estate and the high level of rent arrears which had accumulated over a number of years. According to Captain O'Brien of the Board of Works, Gore Booth was the saviour for most of the people. While he had secured enough food and relief for his own tenants he had been 'pressed also to feed his neighbouring tenants'. O'Brien added, 'What he has done for the part of the county where he resides, has been so well done that it would prove a real blessing to enable him to do more' if the government could assist him. Otherwise the population would be dying 'by fifties'.[45]

Gore Booth's reaction to the crisis was not draconian, but philanthropic as can be seen by the large sums of money he spent on relief. From the summer of 1846 Sir Robert was a major importer and supplier of food. Between August 1846 and July 1847 he imported 2,584 tons of food at a cost of £34,822. Corn was purchased at £13 to £14 a ton and sold to the tenants at £15 to £16. The corn was bought on the open market in New York, Liverpool and Greenock and shipped to Sligo. After January 1847 all of his food imports made a loss and he was subsidizing the cost of the corn. During the Famine the overall net loss to Sir Robert on these transactions was £4,212. The cargo on the *Washington*, which went down at sea, was valued at £1,742, and he also suffered losses in October 1847 when one of his provisions stores at John's Port was burgled and a large quantity of meal and Indian corn stolen.[46] By April 1847 he was selling the imported corn at a loss, and giving much of it free to the most destitute.

Gore Booth was prepared to work with other landlords in the importation of corn so that costs could be reduced. He collaborated with Lords Palmerston and Enniskillen in March 1847 to purchase 200 tons of Indian meal which was then distributed among the most impoverished on the three estates. In May he sold 391 tons of corn to Lord Lorton which he had imported on the *Manchester* and made a profit of £710. This money was probably used to pay for further food that was then distributed among his own tenants.[47] Sir Robert was not only purchasing food to feed the poor, but also seed for planting. In the summer of 1847 he imported 261 tons of seed oats, barley and wheat at a cost of £3,941. This was sold on to his tenants, but at a considerable loss as he received only £1,368.[48]

While Gore Booth was initially prepared to look after the tenants on his estate, he quickly realized that the situation on the adjoining properties of Sir Gilbert King, Capt. Michael Kelly and Charles Gore Jones, was critical and he came to the rescue of these beleaguered people. Being a resident landlord he was aware at first hand of the crisis in north Sligo. Proprietors such as Lord Palmerston, who were absentees, were unable to react as quickly. In 1847, the Revd John Green, the vicar of Ahamlish and secretary of the local relief committee, stated that Palmerston had provided little help and the poorest of his tenants were excluded from the relief works and 'are literally in a state of starvation'.[49] Sir Robert's philanthropy saved many of these people as he was providing them and the Palmerston tenants on Inishmurray Island with relief. In early 1847 half of the population of Ahamlish were starving and within a short period thirty people had died.[50] In January 1847 the *Sligo Champion* reported that the position was deplorable and published lists of those who had died of starvation. Fifteen had died in one week because they had no food. 'Deaths from starvation are now so numerous, that they are looked upon as a matter of course, and have ceased to create alarm, or horror in the public mind.'[51] The Catholic curate of

Grange, Fr Dominick Noone, stated that many of the inhabitants of Ahamlish parish had not eaten one regular meal for three weeks. He named seventeen people, aged between 12 and 68 years, who had died in the parish in late February. By March the mortality rate in Ahamlish was seven a day.[52] Sir Robert verified the chronic state of affairs.

Gore Booth was also providing assistance to the 300 people who lived at 'The Sands' on the north shore of Sligo Bay, where the land had become totally useless because of sea sand sweeping over it for many years. The lands were owned by John Gethan, but Sir Robert distributed bread and medicines two or three times a week, 'to those who must die if food be not given them'. Their condition was such that they were unable to send their children to the public works to earn money. Gore Booth added, 'The distress in this district cannot be imagined, it must be seen, but I am happy to say very little exists on my own property or those portions over which I have control. The human creatures must be kept alive at all costs.'[53] Captain Henry O'Brien, a Board of Works officer, corroborated the accounts when he visited 'The Sands' with Sir Robert in the spring of 1847, stating that dozens of people were dying daily and recalling the statement of one woman, 'It would be better if we were all dead'.[54] Gore Booth was also providing relief for other tenants on the townlands of Ardtarmon, Rughin, Ballintemple and Ballyconnell in the Lissadell electoral division. Only Ardtarmon was part of Sir Robert's estate. Nevertheless, he took on the responsibility of helping the people on all of these townlands.[55] Sir Robert was also providing assistance on other townlands. In October 1847 there were 929 totally destitute people in the Cloonaghill Electoral Division and they did not have a morsel of food. Two families, six individuals, were on the townland of Cloonamahon which was owned by Gore Booth. In Kilturra electoral division, 853 people were destitute and 74 were on the townlands of Knockgrana, Knockgloss and Rathbane, the property of Sir Robert.[56] The problem in these electoral divisions was that the holdings were too small to support the population and they would have been unable to survive even if they were given the lands rent free. Food was needed for survival and this was provided by Gore Booth.

It is difficult to estimate the exact financial cost of Gore Booth's relief operations during the Famine. Contemporary sources put the figure at between £30,000 and £80,000.[57] £40,000 seems more plausible and this does not include the sum that was spent on the assisted emigration schemes.[58] The relief was financed through a number of sources: directly by Sir Robert himself, through contributions from friends and acquaintances, and donations forwarded by the Society of Friends. Throughout the Famine years, Gore Booth, like most other Irish landowners, received little or nothing in rent from his Irish properties.[59] Were it not for the income from his Lancashire estates Gore Booth might have become bankrupt and might have had to sell off some of his lands in the Encumbered Estates Court. In March 1847 Sir Robert stated that he was able to pay for the relief because 'my property being without debt, I can carry on for a little, although it is a hard act to have to burthen [*sic*] ones property with debt for others – but we must keep (the) creatures alive at any cost'.[60] Nevertheless, he was left with repayments on the loan he had taken out to purchase the Ballymote property. As a result he had to mortgage the Lissadell lands in 1847 for £50,000.[61] Contributions totaling £685 towards the relief efforts were also secured from friends and acquaintances. These included £430 from Richard Calridge of Eton, £100 from the prime minister, Lord John Russell, and £5 from Lady Dunraven.[62]

Gore Booth's role in the alleviation of hunger and destitution in the north Sligo region was exceptional compared with the contributions of other local landowners. In the barony of Lyney, Co. Sligo, out of a population of 30,000, 24,000 were destitute, but local landlords only gave employment to 100 or 110 men.[63] Throughout the 1845–50 period the proprietors as a group were condemned and severely criticized for not coming to the aid of the people. In September 1846 the London *Universe* stated that Irish landlords showed a complete selfishness and heartlessness towards the Irish peasants and were heedless of all rebuke.[64] However, in the early stages of the Famine many landowners did provide their tenants with assistance, independent of the government measures. These tended to be proprietors who resided on their Irish estates.[65] Their contributions to the relief committees and the provision of aid was especially important. This changed after 1847 when responsibility for relief was transferred to the poor law unions and landowners saw their poor law rates rise significantly. This was at a time when many were insolvent and receiving no rents. Local relief committees in Co. Sligo were exasperated with the prevarications or refusal of many proprietors to provide assistance. The annual rentals from land in Co. Sligo in the mid-1840s was estimated at £235,756, but the landowners did not provide £2,000 in assistance for the poor between 1845 and 1847. The *Sligo Champion* was adamant that most of the Sligo landlords had done nothing to aid their tenants.[66] The problem was that most of the smaller proprietors in the north Sligo region were in no position to help. By 1845 one landowner in twelve in Ireland was chronically insolvent.[67]

Throughout 1846 and 1847 the nationalist newspaper, the *Sligo Champion*, was severely critical of the landowners in the county stating that they were doing nothing to help the people.[68] Even Gore Booth was attacked in September 1846 for evicting thirty tenants who were in arrears with their rent and who had reoccupied their farms. Sir Robert was criticized for not leaving them in possession until the spring when the tenants would save their crops and be in a better position to leave for America. The *Champion* did not take into consideration Sir Robert's promise to provide alternative arrangements for them.[69] By 1849 the *Champion* had completely changed its attitude towards Gore Booth and extolled his virtues as a proprietor who worked tirelessly not only to look after his own tenants, but also those on neighbouring estates.

Sir Robert's philanthropy was also publicly acknowledged by the parish priest of Drumcliff, Fr Patrick O'Gara, which was most unusual as most of the Catholic clergy were extremely critical of the landlords for their failure to aid their tenants and for the estate clearances they were carrying out. The priests were prepared to denounce landowners from the altar and in some cases publicly named them in newspapers. In March 1848, O'Gara wrote. 'It must be a source of consolation to you, that, whilst other landlords were flying the country through apprehension of personal peril, you were deeply rooted in the affections of a grateful peasantry.'[70] The gratitude can also be noted in that the church clock in Ballymote town was purchased by the tenants of that part of the estate in recognition of Gore Booth's relief efforts during the Famine. The tenants' attitude can also be seen from the memorial that he received from the Lissadell tenants and which still adorns Lissadell House, thanking him for saving the lives of the people. Despite his efforts and the appreciation of the majority of the people of Sligo, Gore Booth received a death threat in early December 1847.[71] Nothing ever came of this and one can only assume that he was targeted simply because he was a landlord.

Irish landlords have been severely criticized for their role during the Famine for two reasons: their overall lack of direct involvement in the relief operations and the large-scale estate clearances they carried out, especially after the Gregory Quarter Acre clause came into being in 1847. It is unfair to categorize all proprietors as having behaved in this way. Sir Robert Gore Booth was not an exterminator and played a major role in the relief operations in north Sligo; working day and night not only to relieve the suffering on his own property, but also on neighbouring estates. Not only was Sir Robert prepared to mortgage his lands to help in the relief of distress, he also worked in a practical way to help the people of the region. He accompanied government officials, journalists and others to those villages where destitution and famine were rampant, in the hope that they might be able to secure additional aid for the poor. Gore Booth was annoyed with the government for blaming the landlords for not coming to the aid of the people, and he was angry because the proprietors had to shoulder the intolerable poor law rates. By late 1847 he realized that the crisis could not be contained by individual effort. Direct government involvement was needed, but the authorities continued to insist that Irish land must pay for the relief even though the country was not in a position to take on this responsibility. Throughout the Famine years Gore Booth had only one aim: to save the people from starvation. He sought no public recognition or accolades. In an undated letter during the Famine, Sir Robert said that he did not want his charitable work brought before the public, 'I do what I considered only my duty, and I have at all times endeavoured to do the same, therefore I do not wish nor care to be vindicated in any way as an Irish landlord.'[72] His avoidance of publicity meant that no accounts of his relief activities featured in the local or national newspapers before 1847.

3. The assisted emigration schemes

Prior to the Famine, Sir Roger Gore Booth had introduced remedial measures to make his Co. Sligo properties viable and profitable. A central feature of this policy was assisting his tenants to emigrate to North America. He was among a handful of landowners who initiated emigration schemes from their properties in the 1830s: paying the passage fares, providing clothing and provisions for the boat journey and in some cases the landing money when they arrived at the North America ports, money which could be used to bring the emigrants to their final destinations. A number of proprietors in pre-Famine Ireland saw emigration as the panacea to the problems of destitution, congestion and famine on their estates, but only a few, such as Gore Booth, the Wandesfordes in Co. Kilkenny and Col. George Wyndham in Co. Clare had the vision and determination to implement this policy before the Great Famine.[1] Gore Booth and the others were influenced by the suggestions and recommendations that were being put forward in the 1820s and 1830s regarding the alleviation of destitution and under-employment in the country. These included relief schemes, the development of the fishing industry, the improvement of the road network and assisted emigration.[2] However, some proprietors felt there was little point in putting money into relief efforts within Ireland as it would not solve the fundamental problem of destitution and overpopulation. It was estimated that in the worst congested regions of the country up to one-sixth of the population needed to be taken off the land so that the rest of the population would be able to survive.[3]

The ending of the rundale system caused problems on the Gore Booth estate as it created a surplus landless population who could no longer be accommodated. Sir Robert decided that the only way to help these people was to provide them with the financial assistance to leave for North America. Those who refused were offered financial compensation or holdings on other parts of the estate.[4] He had the option of evicting the surplus tenantry, as many other proprietors were doing, but felt this was uncharitable and in June 1848 told the House of Lords Select Committee on Colonization that if he did this, 'I should have been throwing them on the world and leaving them to beg.'[5] This was one of the main reasons he introduced assisted emigration in 1834. In that year Martin's lease at Ballygilgan came into Gore Booth's possession. As the townland was grossly congested with many sub-tenants on small, unviable holdings who had to supplement their income through fishing, he decided to consolidate the farms into one holding.

Forty-two families, comprising 207 individuals, accepted Sir Robert's offer of assisted passage in 1839 and 1841 and received potatoes and other provisions for the sea journey.[6] A number of large families were part of this group: Patrick Mulvaney had ten in family; Patrick Haye also had ten, George Feeney had nine, Martin Feeney had eleven and Daniel McGowan had eight.[7]

As most small holders and labourers did not have the financial resources to emigrate it was imperative that proprietors like Sir Robert provided the assistance. It would cost in the region of £15 for a labourer to emigrate with his wife and three children, and this was as much as he would earn in a year. Unless he was removed he would become dependent on the landlord, either through maintenance in the workhouse or on the estate. It was also important that the poorer tenants left and not the prosperous and well off. Poor tenants were a financial liability and a 'deadweight', and cost the landowner money, while the prosperous tenants had a part to play in the economic improvement of the estate and were more likely to be able to pay their rents. The tenants who were selected for emigration tended to be small farmers whose holdings were unviable. Often they had secured their plots of land from middlemen and larger tenant farmers, against the landlord's wishes. As a result proprietors such as Gore Booth targeted these tenants.

There were three main reasons why landlords such as Gore Booth initiated assisted emigration schemes. First, it improved the estate's economic position by allowing the creation of more viable holdings. Second, proprietors would have been forced to pay for the upkeep of the pauper population either by buying in food or contributing to their upkeep in the workhouses. This was especially the situation after the Irish Poor Law was introduced in 1838. Third, it was felt that removing the poorest would reduce the level of outrages and lawlessness on estates. Congestion and poverty, it was claimed, led to high levels of crime and lawlessness as the people were underemployed.[8] Joseph Kincaid, Lord Palmerston's agent, felt that emigration was the remedy for the lawlessness that existed on many overpopulated properties.[9] While Sir Robert pursued assisted emigration to clear the estate of the surplus population, he also availed of the opportunity to get rid of tenants whom he regarded as undesirable and of 'bad character'. He 'helped' those who were of an indifferent character or who were 'in the habit of making whisky, or of a doubtful character'. Gore Booth preferred to see such individuals leave rather than 'getting rid of a good respectable tenant'.[10] However, he did not appear to worry how such 'bad characters' would be received in North America.

Certain rules and procedures were adopted. Like most other landowners involved in assisted emigration, Gore Booth ensured entire families were aided and he was reluctant to help individuals or parts of families as this would not alleviate the problems of congestion and unviable holdings. Of the hundred people sent to St John, New Brunswick on the *Lady Sale* in

July 1847, nearly all were families, as with James Murphy, his wife and seven children who ranged in age from 25 to 10 years, and Widow McGlone who was accompanied by her five children, ranging in age from 25 to 18.[11] Once the families left the estate their homes were immediately pulled down. The tenants who were assisted from Ballygilgan between 1834 and 1839 were paid to demolish their houses.[12] This earned the tenant some money and ensured that squatters would not take possession of the vacated holdings.

One of the principal features of the private emigration schemes was that those who financed them felt they had the right to choose the emigrants.[13] Selected emigration was felt to be more beneficial than unplanned emigration. Gore Booth was prepared to send old people, and widows and orphans, as in the case of Widow McGlone, because they were unlikely to undertake permanent improvements on their holdings.

Some argued that while such emigration was a necessary remedy to improve the country it had to be organized and not pursued in an unplanned way. Individuals mainly left when emigration was unplanned: often they were the more able and enterprising members of the community. The poor and less industrious people stayed behind. It was also argued that the unplanned emigration of families resulted in large amounts of capital being taken out of the country. With planned emigration remittances were sent back to Ireland quickly.

It was important that the first group of assisted emigrants was a success as the continuance of further schemes depended on their favourable reports. In the early stages little information was available as to the suitability of destinations so that the first groups were often the pioneers. While Gore Booth and other proprietors could provide information on the advantages of settlement in North America, the types of skills that were required and the wage levels available, reports in a letter from a friend or relation did more to promote emigration. Thus the emigration agent was not the landowner or the government, but other emigrants. Fear of the unknown was a major obstacle in establishing successful emigration patterns and this was the main reason why some of the Ballygilgan tenants decided to take the plots of lands on other parts of the Gore Booth estate rather than go to an unknown destination in North America. They were reluctant to depart because they knew nothing about the new world. They were ill-informed and unprepared. Thus the emigrants' letters were the main impetus in enticing friends and relations to come to North America. These letters confirmed the image of a 'promized land of plenty'. This was very important for the emigration of the poorer classes. It was often the initial push that was the crucial factor in initiating the chain migration of the poorer classes and in encouraging them to seek assistance in subsequent emigration schemes. Once favourable accounts and remittances were sent back by the Gore Booth tenants who had been assisted in the late 1830s there was a steady demand from others for assistance.

Women were particularly receptive to the prospects of a new life in North America, as borne out in many letters that Sir Robert received. It is also probably a factor why many of the assisted families were headed by women. While men had a bond with the land and were reluctant to sever this attachment, women took a more pragmatic approach. They were the ones who struggled with starvation, the uncertainty associated with crop failures and subsistence crises, and were happy to leave behind this subsistence existence. It was more difficult encourage people to leave for the colonies when sufficient food was available. Many were reluctant to leave the holdings into which they had been born.[14] Sir Robert told the House of Lords Select Committee on Colonization from Ireland in 1847 that the tenants 'have a very strong affection for the ground they have resided upon, and would in many instances, prefer existing upon it to getting rich elsewhere'. They disliked moving, even to other parts of the estate, and did so only when there was no other option.[15] Only when the potato failed and famine became a reality did the people look for assistance to leave.

While Sir Robert initiated the emigration in 1834, the schemes were not 'estate-driven' as on many other properties: where the tenants themselves asked to be sent to North America, especially after 1845. Gore Booth was at pains to stress that coercion was not used. While many were reluctant to take up the landlord's offer before 1845, this changed during the Famine years. In June 1848, Sir Robert told the House of Lord Select Committee on Colonization the he never compelled an individual to emigrate, 'If a man could not go back to his own farm, he had the choice of going to another farm – inferior ground, but a significant quantity for his needs. No man was compelled to go by me.'[16] The voluntary nature of the emigration was backed up by the parish priest of Drumcliff, Fr Patrick O'Gara, who in 1848 said that the emigration was entirely voluntary: no compulsion had ever been used and the emigrants had always been well cared for.[17] During the Famine years, many realized that their immediate fate was starvation and possibly death. As a result the tenants were more receptive to settlement in North America and emigration now became 'tenant-driven'. Gore Booth tried to accommodate as many as possible, but the demand was such that he could not help everybody. This can be seen on the *Aeolus* when sixteen stowaways from the estate were discovered when the ship arrived in St John, New Brunswick, in June 1847.[18] As has already been noted in chapter 2, Sir Robert faced a cash crisis during the Famine years and while the numbers applying for assistance increased, rents were declining. There were also increased demands on his financial resources as he was providing relief for the starving populations of Lissadell and Ballymote.

While other landowners, such as Lords Palmerston and Lansdowne, left the planning and organization of their migration schemes to their agents, Sir Robert was directly involved in all aspects of the emigration from his estate.[19] He took a great interest in the emigrants' welfare from the moment they left the property up to their arrival in North America. Landowners who were associated with such emigration over a period of time and who carefully planned the schemes tended to look after their emigrants rather better than those who had a knee-jerk reaction to the Famine crisis. The tenants were examined twice by Sir Robert's physician, Dr Hamilton, before they left for Canada: first at Lissadell when the emigrants were given clothing and bedding. The second examination occurred at Sligo before the emigrants embarked. A number of emigrants were not allowed to travel when it was discovered they had fever.[20] The Gore Booth accounts for 1847 show that he provided bread, Indian meal, whole meal and flour for the tenants who sailed on the *Aeolus, Yeoman* and *Scrouge* at a total cost of £300. Passengers had a different diet every day and also got tea and sugar. In addition, Lady Gore Booth provided £140 worth of clothing and blankets and £10 for the poorer emigrants. The passengers on the *Yeoman* were also given a cow so that fresh milk was available on the journey.[21] Sir Robert also gave instructions that if provisions were left over after disembarkation it should be distributed amongst the needy emigrants.[22] He also applied to the government through the Irish lord lieutenant, Lord Bessborough, for a grant of waste lands in Canada to which his tenants could be sent. Gore Booth asked the government to provide each tenant with one hundred acres of land, or allow them to pay for their farms through instalments. Sir Roger was prepared to pay for an agent to travel with the emigrants and support them at his own expense for the first year.[23] The authorities refused this request, an indication of the government's overall ambivalence towards assisted emigration. While it had been suggested in the 1820s and 1830s that joint government-landlord ventures be put in place the authorities refused to take an active role.[24] Gore Booth was never happy with the government prevarication towards assisted emigration.

Gore Booth also wrote to the Canadian authorities asking them to support his emigrants. During 1847 he informed the emigration agent for St John, John Robinson, when the ships carrying his tenants were due to arrive at the port and requested they be given whatever aid they needed. One of Robinson's main functions was to secure employment for the new arrivals and he appears to have carried out this work diligently although his task was made more onerous by the emigrants' high expectations, especially regarding wages. There were occasions during 1847 when Robinson was exasperated by the emigrants' demands. Nevertheless, he successfully secured employment for many of the new arrivals and in August 1847 sent 150 of the *Yeoman* passengers to Fredericton and thirty to Digby.[25] The New Brunswick authorities did whatever they could for the Gore Booth emigrants but were overwhelmed by the number of destitute Irish that arrived at St John during that year and did not have the resources to cope.

The level of assisted emigration depended on the amount that landowners were prepared to spend. Landowners who were prepared to look after their tenants properly found that it was an expensive exercise. Most proprietors attempted to keep expenditure to a minimum. They did this by chartering a boat, sometimes in association with other landlords. During 1847 Sir Robert teamed up with his neighbour, Lord Palmerston, to send out tenants on the *Lady Sale* and the *Aeolus*. From the available evidence from those estates that assisted emigrants during the Famine, landlord expenditure never exceeded £5 per person.[26] The cost of the emigration from the Gore Booth estate between 1834 and 1848 was £6,720, of which £5,999 was spent during 1847 and 1848. The cost per person between 1835 and 1842 worked out at £3 and for 1847–8 between £4 and £4 15s. It cost £1,600 to send 386 people on the *Aeolus* in 1847, not including expenditure on extra provisions, clothing or the landing money given to the emigrants when they disembarked. The 396 passengers who left on the *Yeoman* cost Sit Robert £2,300, while the *Lady Sale* had 340 passengers and £2,036 was expended.[27] No landowner, regardless of his wealth, could afford to expend such large sums especially when they were receiving little rent. This was one of the reasons why Sir Robert conducted the schemes in phases over a number of years, although most expenditure occurred during 1847. Between 1834 and 1848 Gore Booth assisted 1,500 people to emigrate. The Gore Booth emigration was not financed from the rentals from his Sligo properties, but from the money he received from his Lancashire properties.[28] He was also forced to borrow for the schemes and his Lancashire properties provided the collateral.[29]

To minimize his costs Sir Robert, like most other landowners engaged in assisting their tenants to emigrate, sent his tenants to Canada. Passage costs were cheaper to the Canadian colonies than to the United States: in 1835 a ticket from Drogheda to Quebec cost £2, while the fare to New York was £4 and this did not include bed and provisions. From Derry port it cost £4 10s. to the United States and from 30s. to £2 to Quebec.[30] Fares to the United States were more expensive because the ships masters had to pay a bond to ensure that none of their passengers became a public charge and the captain faced a year in jail or forfeit of his vessel for carrying passengers above the legal limit allowed. The vessels that travelled between Canada and Ireland tended to carry timber and other goods and returned with a human cargo as ballast. Canada thus became a major destination for Irish emigrants and at least 450,000 disembarked there between 1825 and 1845, although many subsequently settled in the United States. Canada was also favoured because it was the closest British colony to Ireland.

By the 1830s St John, New Brunswick, had become one of the most important disembarkation points for Irish emigrants to British North America. Many landowners were happy to use the port as a point of entry for their emigrants to North America. Sir Robert Gore Booth sent his emigrants to this destination, indicating his desire to keep costs to a minimum. Like many others, the Gore Booth emigrants headed for the United States. Moses H. Perley, the emigration officer for New Brunswick, found that only one in eight of the newly arrived emigrants remained in the colony.[31] For most emigrants Canada was just the disembarkation point in their journey towards settlement in the United States. The lure of the American economy was irresistable and they were drawn to the cities along the east coast. Emigrants to British North America needed to arrive in the colonies during the summer, especially if they sought agricultural work. This allowed those who wanted to take up land the opportunity to make provision for themselves for the winter months. It was felt that May to August was the best period for such emigrants to arrive in Canada.[32]

The experiences of the Gore Booth emigrants on the journey to New Brunswick mirrored those of many others that were sent to North America. A committee of the tenants who sailed on the *Aeolus* that arrived at St John on 31 May 1847, issued a statement which said that Sir Robert was 'always kind to his tenants; it was not tyranny which forced us to emigrate – it was the loss of our crops for two years past and we hope to gain a living in America by strict industry and sobriety'. They expressed their gratitude to Sir Robert and the captain of the *Aeolus*, Michael Driscoll, for the way they were dealt with during the crossing, stating that Driscoll had treated the passengers well and distributed the provisions fairly.[33] Two persons died on the trip, Mrs Connolly and Mr McGowan; and five children died as the boat lay at St John, Sally Toger, aged 18; Unity Burns, 11 years; Patrick Crade, 7 years; Biddy Kilbane, 15 years and Mary Hartt.[34] Those who received extra provisions from landowners like Gore Booth for the Atlantic crossing were in a much better state than most other passengers. Steerage travellers were expected to bring their own food and cook it on the few grates that were provided. If the journey took longer than expected these passengers had to survive as best they could.[35]

The experiences of the other boats that carried Gore Booth's emigrants during 1847 were not as favourable as those on the *Aeolus*. The *Yeoman*, which had 503 passengers, arrived at St John on 19 August 1847 after a 34 day journey from Sligo. Two people died on the trip, one a 60-year old woman, and sixty people caught the dreaded Famine fever. Ten were in a severe state and one died. After arriving at St John five infants and one adult died of fever.[36] According to one passenger, Richard Yeates, most arrived at the port in a reasonable state because of the care and attention of the ship captain, John Purden, and his wife 'whose attention throughout the voyage to all was beyond anything I should have imagined and for theirs to me I cannot ever forget'.[37] However, the experience of those on the *Yeoman* was quite different. After fifteen days at sea, Patt McGowan contacted the fever from another passenger and was in a poor condition for the next three weeks. After arriving at St John he was sent to the quarantine station at Partridge Island where for three days he passed blood. He spent five weeks at the quarantine station before he was discharged and went to St John. Shortly afterwards he relapsed and spent over eight weeks in the fever hospital.[38] Eight of the *Aeolus* passengers died of fever at sea and another 28 lay dangerously ill on board, some of whom died shortly after their arrival at St John.[39]

The contrasting experiences of the Gore Booth passengers is indicative of the difficulties which the Famine emigrants faced. While Sir Robert provided adequate provisions and they were well looked after on the crossing, they arrived in St John in a wretched state because of fever. Nobody could state categorically why the fever occurred on one boat resulting in high mortality, but not on another.

While Michael Driscoll and others gave impressive accounts of the passengers' voyages to St John it masked the problems which beset the emigrants from the time of their arrival at the port. Sir Robert provided for the emigrants up to their disembarkation, but only then did the trauma that they faced become apparent. The St John authorities were unable to cope with the large influx of Irish Famine paupers, not only from the Gore Booth estate, but also from other properties such as those of Lords Fitzwilliam and Palmerston. This inability to deal with the thousands of emigrants led to widespread criticism of all landlord emigration schemes. The basic problem was that once the emigrants arrived at St John they had to fend for themselves.

The immediate concern was the appearance of the dreaded typhus, or as it was more commonly known 'Famine fever'. While the boats left the Irish ports without a trace of the disease it could quickly make its appearance and spread rapidly through the passengers. When the *Yeoman* left Sligo on 13 July all of the passengers were reported to be healthy and had been examined by Sir Robert's physician, Dr Hamilton. By the time the boat arrived at St John thirty cases of fever had been reported.[40] However, the main criticism now was not the emigrants' medical condition, but rather the caliber of person that Gore Booth was sending. What was particularly worrying was the large numbers of females that were arriving at St John. When the *Lady Sale* disembarked on 9 September, with 412 passengers, 200 from the Palmerston and 150 from the Gore Booth estates, there was a high proportion of women and children, and elderly men, and they were not properly clothed. There were 176 adult females, nine were widows, and 57 children, including a number of orphans. It is not possible to discern how many came from the Gore Booth estate. The emigration agent at St John stated, 'I have never yet seen such abject misery, destitution and helplessness as was exhibited yesterday on the decks of the *Lady Sale*.'[41] Another problem was the large number of children dependent on one adult. In one case sixteen children accompanied one man who was probably their grandfather. As far as the New Brunswick authorities were concerned the poor and destitute had been forced to leave Sligo and it was suggested that Gore Booth was displacing such people to reduce his poor rate liability. This attitude was reinforced when a further group of passengers from the Gore Booth and Palmerston estates arrived at St John on the *Aeolus* on 31 October. W.H. Harding, the Health Officer at the port, reported that 99 out of every 100 passengers would have to be supported by public charity for the immediate future. He stated many were old, others 'with broken down constitutions, and subjects of chronic diseases, lame widows with very helpless families; in fact all those causes which rendered them paupers upon the lands of their landlords'. Harding expressed dismay that any landowner would send out so many paupers, 'who so tame would not feel indignant at the outrage'.[42]

The question has to be asked: why the sudden transformation in 1847 from a situation where the emigrants arrived in a good condition to that where they became an immediate burden on the New Brunswick authorities? A plausible explanation is the pressure that Sir Robert was under from tenants who wished to leave during the summer of 1847. They were so intent on escaping famine and destitution that they wanted immediate assistance, and as has already been noted the demand was greater than the supply. Gore Booth in his attempt to accommodate them did not always ensure that the most suitable applicants were selected. Lack of preparation can also be noted in that the latter emigrants arrived at St John in September and late October 1847 at a time when they were unable to make arrangements for themselves for the winter months. These later groups tarnished Gore Booth's reputation. The fact that most emigrants were properly looked after, from the time that emigration was first introduced in 1834, was not acknowledged by the New Brunswick authorities. Moses Perley was convinced that Gore Booth was getting rid of his helpless paupers and they were being exported to disencumber the estate.[43] Sir Robert was also being condemned because of the appalling state in which all of the assisted emigrants arrived at St John in 1847.[44]

While Gore Booth was receiving reports that most of the emigrants had disembarked in a good condition, it was clear that they were not prepared for life in North America. The number of former Gore Booth tenants who became a charge on the New Brunswick authorities was evidence of their poor preparation. Despite John Driscoll's assertion that the emigrants on the *Aeolus* were well looked after, seventy-two passengers were admitted to the St John's Almshouse at Courtney Bay because they were destitute. In some cases it was only for a few weeks: Margaret Currie was admitted on 29 June 1847 and discharged on 13 July, and Paddy Carthy was incarcerated between 29 June and 12 July. Others were admitted for longer periods: Denis Calone spent from 24 June to 24 August in the almshouse. In some instances whole families were admitted because they were destitute, as with James Galoon and his five children aged between eight and 20 years, who were inmates between 8 and 15 July. Adam Johnson and his four children, ranging in age from four to 16 years, were admitted on 21 July. Five emigrants died there: James Conroy, Margaret Gallagher, Bridget Harkins, Mary McGolderick and Anne Kearins.[45] In addition 40 passengers on the boat were orphaned children and were sent to the emigrant orphan asylum in St John.[46]

The circumstances of the emigrants who arrived on the *Aeolus* on its second voyage on 31 October were even more alarming; 172 passengers had to be admitted to the St John hospital almshouse over the following twelve months; 15 died there including two sisters, Honora and Margaret Cronin, aged 10 and 12 years. Even more revealing was the large numbers of passengers who were being constantly admitted to the almshouse, such as Thomas Pye who was 50 years and was admitted on 20 March 1848 and finally discharged on 21 July. William Pye, probably his son and aged 23, was an inmate in the institution for the same period. Another feature was the number of young, able-bodied people who were admitted; 86 were between 15 and 30 years, indicating the difficulty in securing employment and that many were physically unfit for work.[47] Not all were from the Gore Booth estate as a large number were from the Palmerston estate and it is difficult determine who came from each estate. Between March and November 1847 a total of 619 people were admitted to the almshouse and Thomas Power suggests that a large proportion were passengers on the *Aeolus* and *Lady Sale*, and originated from the Palmerston and Gore Booth properties; 269 of these inmates were women, 194 men and 156 children.[48]

The problem was compounded when parents left their children in the St John Orphan Asylum and headed to the United States in search of work, returning for their children when their circumstances improved. A recent study shows that 47 per cent of the orphans admitted into the orphanage in 1847 were from Co. Sligo, suggesting that many were probably from the Gore Booth estate.[49] In December 1847 the St John authorities were still discussing the level of vagrancy and mendacity among the Gore Booth emigrants and it was stated 'the presence of so many idle people in this city has given occasion to much apprehension of disturbances'.

Criticism cannot be directed exclusively at Sir Robert since, according to the St John authorities, the emigrants themselves were not prepared to improve their position. Gore Booth was giving them the opportunity, but they were not availing of the chance to better themselves. Sir Robert admitted that some were sent who were 'idle, lazy fellows who never would improve nor do good anywhere'.[50] While the landlord asked the Hon. John Robertson to secure work for the new arrivals this was not always possible. It was reported that many paupers started begging immediately after disembarkation and this led to local resentment.[51] The emigrants on the *Lady Sale* and the second *Aeolus* group were difficult to accommodate as 'they are utterly ignorant of the work here and unless they take less wages than those accustomed to the work they are not employed'. John Robertson told Henry Gore Booth that the emigrants sought higher wages than they were entitled to, were a difficult people to manage and as a result were unemployed. Those who were prepared to work for lower wages or were prepared to move inland could expect reasonable jobs.[52] The problem was that most of the emigrants did not have the money to move beyond St John. Many had high expectations because of the letters they received from friends and relations who had already settled in North America and who intimated that wages were good. They now refused to work for 3s. 4d. per day. The Gore Booth emigrants were not aware of the downturn in the colony's economic fortunes leading to a scarcity in employment opportunities and wage reductions. Robertson's exasperation with the *Yeoman* and *Lady Sale* emigrants can be seen in his statement that he wished 'that she might bring some other cargo'. New Brunswick employers were reluctant to employ the newly arrived emigrants because of their fear of contacting the Famine fever. Some of the emigrants, for example Thomas Bowes, were also involved in crime and lawlessness. Bowes had sailed on the *Aeolus* and was accused of killing a Mr Briggs in Portland, New Brunswick. The Irish emigrant community was not prepared to assist the local authorities despite a £250 reward for Bowes' capture.[53]

As pressure mounted on the New Brunswick authorities regarding the destitute Famine emigrants it was inevitable that landowners like Gore Booth were severely criticised. This was reflected in an editorial in the *St John Courier* which attacked the way that Irish emigrants were left in the colony and complained that unless action was taken the aged and infirm emigrants would have to be supported long term by public charity.[54] Adam Ferrie, chairman of the Emigration Committee, was extremely critical of landowners such as Sir Robert, and stated, 'I must … express my deep regret that men pretending to be Christian, and especially British, could be guilty of such barbarity, evidently for the paltry purpose of freeing themselves from the natural and just burden of assisting to support and provide for their poor.'[55] He compared the situation to the slave trade and felt it would have been better to deprive these people of life at once rather than subject them to the 'extreme suffering and privations which they had to endure'. Moses H. Perley was convinced that Sir Robert was 'shovelling out' his helpless paupers and some would remain a permanent charge on the colony. He added that such emigration should 'be publicly noted and condemned'.[56] A resolution from the Common Council of St John followed on 3 September expressing the apprehension and alarm which the city had to withstand because of the large influx of 'pauper Irish emigrants'. The resolution was scathing of the Irish landlords who were 'shipping ship-loads of paupers from their respective estates for the purpose of relieving themselves from their undoubted and legitimate liability of providing the requisite support'. It was felt that the landlords were transferring the burden of support onto the Canadian provinces.[57] A further resolution was passed in November 1847 by the council, largely as a result of the condition of the Gore Booth passengers who arrived on the *Aeolus* on 31 October 1847. It stated that the city was already burdened with destitute poor and all the available places in the almshouse were filled with pauper Irish. It threatened to return the Gore Booth emigrants to Ireland, not because of their anxiety about the destitute passengers, but because they were angry with Sir Robert for having sent such unsuitable persons to their shores.[58] These resolutions reflected the overall attitude of the local community.

Such criticisms resulted in the Colonial and Emigration Commissioners, based in London, expressing their concern about the actions of Gore Booth and those other landlords who sent out the old, widows and children to New Brunswick. In a statement in November 1847 the commissioners said, 'far from the colonies being a fit asylum for the weak, an emigrant requires even more than the average of health and strength to succeed, and consequently, that when they are assisted to go, it is equally unjust to the British provinces, and cruel to the poor persons themselves, to send out those who are totally unable to live by their own industry'.[59]

Gore Booth and the other landlords were very sensitive to such hostile criticisms. Sir Robert maintained that government inaction in providing waste lands in Canada created the problems. When the authorities did not respond to his request he was forced to let the emigrants 'shift for themselves' and they had contracted fever, 'from the want of proper attendance and judicious arrangements at the quarantine stations'.[60]

The Emigration Commissioners, as a result of the criticisms of Gore Booth and other landowners, set guidelines regarding emigration. These stated that those who were coming to the North American colonies should be only those who would succeed and strongly recommended that the emigrants should arrive in North America during the summer months. In March 1848 the New Brunswick authorities passed legislation imposing a levy of between 10s. and 20s. on each emigrant entering the province. In addition, the ship master had to pay 5s. for each passenger that was placed in the quarantine station at Partridge Island.[61] This action greatly curtailed the emigration activities of landlords such as Gore Booth.

What was the attitude of the Gore Booth emigrants regarding their situation in New Brunswick? Their feelings towards Sir Robert varied greatly. Some were unhappy with the decision to leave Sligo because they were unemployed in New Brunswick or had contracted fever. Bryan Clancy who arrived on the *Aeolus* could not get work and in November 1847 told his mother that he was without a job and he 'offten [*sic*] wished to be at home again bad and all as it were. We often wished we never saw St John'. He was happy that one of his sisters had not come to North America because many who had travelled with them had died. His disillusionment with his situation can be seen when he wrote, 'if either boy or girl had any sort of good service it would be better than here'.[62]

Others regarded their emigration as an opportunity to improve themselves and were appreciative of Sir Robert's role. Eliza Quin, when writing to her parents in January 1848, enquired as to how Sir Robert and his family were and asked 'to return Lady Gore my kind compliments for her kindness to me'.[63] Similar sentiments were also expressed by many of the passengers on the *Aeolus* and the *Lady Sale*. Most were happy with their new lives in North America. Catherine Bradley, who settled in St John, wrote back to Sligo within six weeks of her arrival, urging her friends and relatives to join her in the colony.[64] While they were happy to have left famine and destitution behind, they were still concerned about those family members who remained in Sligo, as with Bryan Clancy and John Mullowney. They felt they were lucky and wished to help those back in Ireland and were adamant that they would remit money as soon as they could.[65] These letters, both positive and negative, were given by Gore Booth to the House of Lords Select Committee on Colonization in 1847.

The evualation of the impact of emigration on the Gore Booth tenants must not be confined to their experiences on board the ships and in the immediate period after of their arrival. It has to be analysed in terms of their long-term progress. Like many other emigrants to St John the majority did not settle in New Brunswick, but headed for destinations in the United States. 1848 saw an economic downturn in New Brunswick, especially within the timber trade. Consequently, employment opportunities were few and many of the Gore Booth emigrants headed for New York and New England. Those who moved on tended to be the strongest and more industrious; the poor and weak remained in the colony where they continued to be a long-term burden on local charity. Labourers and unskilled workers remained in New Brunswick, settling in King's Ward and the Duke's/ Queen's districts of St John. The Gore Booth emigrants were also to be found in St James, Norton, St David, Fredericton, Studholm, St Patrick, Pennfield and St Andrew's areas.[66] Mary Feeney and her brother, Roger, got jobs at Mispeek, about ten miles from St John. Their neighbours from Sligo, John Mullowney, and his two sisters were close by at Mesbeck, where they worked as domestic servants. Others who travelled on the *Aeolus* got positions as domestic servants in the Fredericton area, earning 15s. to 20s. a month. Others worked as dressmakers.[67] Some heads of households left New Brunswick for Boston, Maine and Vermont, but their families remained in St John and other towns in New Brunswick. Travel to Boston was expensive and not all family members could afford to go. Thus fathers and sons left for the United States, hoping that they would be able to remit money back so that other family members could join them. Some of the Gore Booth tenants did not want to remain in New Brunswick because they feared they would contract the fever. The Henigans who went to Maine said, 'We left miserable St John. It is almost as bad as Ireland. We are getting on very well since we came to the state of Maine.'[68] Employment opportunities in Maine were good, especially on the railroad, with wages of up to 4s. a day during the summer and 3s. a day during the winter.[69]

The evidence of the Gore Booth emigrants who came to New Brunswick in 1847 indicates they were transient. While they disembarked at St John and some settled there, many moved to the United States immediately. By 1848 they had settled in such centres as New Davenport, Massachusetts; Hollowell and Augusta, Maine; Boston and Five Points, New York. These included Eliza Quin, who by January 1848 had settled at 35 Orange Street in New York with her cousin, Edward Quinn, and his wife. Another, Mary McBride first went to Boston but by 1848 had settled in Newbury Port, 45 miles from Boston.[70]

Five Points, situated in the Sixth Ward, Lower Manhattan, had one of the largest clusters of Gore Booth emigrants. It was one of the most decrepit and crime-ridden slums in North America regarded as a virtual no-go area.[71] It had one of the highest concentrations of emigrants sent out by Irish landlords to North America with tenants from the Palmerston, Lansdowne and Gore Booth estates. The emigrants settled here because accommodation was cheap. Most of the Irish inhabitants worked as unskilled labourers on building sites or on the loading and unloading of ships. Women supplemented the family income by taking in lodgers or working as washer women. The Irish were clannish and tended to live in close proximity to the relatives and friends of people they had known in Ireland. The marriage records for the Church of the Transfiguration in Five Points for 1853–5 shows that many of the former Gore Booth emigrants married people who had been their neighbours in Sligo as with Patrick O'Brien who married Bridget Gillen, both from Drumcliff; and Michael Dannellon and Mary Conway also from Drumcliff.[72] They brought with them from Ireland strong social and community bonds. These connections were important during crises such as sickness or financial difficulties. Most of the Gore Booth emigrants settled in the Bottle Alley area of Five Points where they were close to former neighbours from Ahamlish who had been sent out by Lord Palmerston.[73] Here they lived frugally, but being thrifty and bringing with them from Sligo survival techniques they bettered themselves as in evident from the level of savings they deposited with the Emigrant Savings Bank.

Most of the Gore Booth emigrants did not forget the friends and relatives they left in Sligo and like most Irish emigrants to North America their money became an important source of funding for those who stayed at home. Once they adjusted to their new situation and were able to earn a living they remitted sums of money to Sligo. Between 1850 and 1855 Irish emigrants to North America sent an average of £1.2 million annually back to Ireland.[74] In their first letter from St John, John, Mary and Margaret Nancy Mullowney informed their parents in Lissadell that they would send money home as soon as they could.[75] While it is difficult to quantify the level of remittances from the Gore Booth emigrants, it is known that the emigrants from the nearby Palmerston property sent £2,000 back to their relatives in the two years after their arrival in North America.[76] In 1848 Sir Robert stated that a sizeable sum had been remitted to Sligo by those who had been sent out in 1847 so that their friends and relatives could join them in North America.[77]

In 1848 Sir Robert suspended the assisted emigration schemes from his estate, even though many tenants still wanted to leave for North America. There were a number of reasons for this decision. First, he was receiving very little in rent from his Irish estates and could no longer finance the emigration. Second, the New Brunswick authorities' decision to introduce a passenger levy for each emigrant arriving in the colony made the schemes more expensive. Third, the negative reaction to his schemes in North America made them contentious and Sir Robert was unhappy with such condemnations. In November 1847 the Colonial Land and Emigration Commissioners wrote to Sir Robert regarding the criticisms of the St John authorities. While they did state that many of the ships carrying the Gore Booth emigrants had ample provisions for the passengers, there was a feeling that the tenants were 'exported' by the landlord to 'disencumber' his estate and many would 'in all probability become a permanent charge on the public funds'. Sir Robert no longer had the support of the New Brunswick authorities and this was probably the principal factor in Sir Robert's decision to discontinue the emigration schemes.

Gore Booth's assisted emigration schemes remain a matter of controversy and criticism. Recent work by a local historian, Joe McGowan, maintains that the schemes were in effect 'famine clearances' and the emigrants were sent out in coffin ships.[78] Such a statement is too sweeping, based on selective information from the *Lady Sale* and the second *Aeolus* trip and disregards the organization and selection process that Sir Robert put in place when sending out his tenants. It also neglects the positive reports from the New Brunswick officials regarding the passengers that arrived on the first *Aeolus* trip. It fails to take into account those emigrants' letters expressing their gratitude towards Sir Robert for what he had done. Terry Coleman in his work describes Gore Booth as a 'shoveller-out' who expelled his paupers.[79] This criticism also fails to realise that the emigration during 1847 was mainly 'tenant-driven' and the alternative was to evict the tenants, leaving them without hope for the future. In March 1848, Gore Booth said that the desire to leave in 1847 was so great that he could not accommodate everybody and many were refused.[80] At least they faced a better future in North America. Sir Robert showed greater benevolence towards his tenants through these schemes than most other Irish proprietors. However, he must be censured for not having a greater concern for the emigrants after they arrived in New Brunswick.

While his detractors have portrayed Gore Booth as heartless and cruel, this fails to take into account his overall responsibilities. He had to ensure the economic survival of his Sligo property and this could only be achieved through a radical overhaul of the estate which ended congestion and subdivision, and created economic holdings. He demonstrated a certain compassion by giving these tenants an opportunity of starting afresh in a new land. The alternative was eviction and the workhouse. Where Gore Booth was guilty was that adequate provisions were not made for those tenants after disembarkation. He relied on others to provide this aid, but during 1847 the New Brunswick authorities lacked the resources to provide the necessary help. Nevertheless, assisted emigration was important for these people as it gave them the chance to escape famine and death. Most could not afford the fares and would definitely have been destitute if they remained in Sligo.

Gore Booth's emigration schemes differed from many of the other landlord schemes in that they were carried out over an extended period of time. The structures that were in place in 1839 and 1841 were reactivated in 1847. They were well coordinated and planned, indicating a genuine desire to look after the tenants up to their arrival in North America.

To what extent was Sir Robert's assisted emigration project a success? The objective of clearing the estate of the surplus population was achieved and it led to the holdings becoming viable. The Lissadell estate was in much better shape when the Great Famine occurred than were neighbouring properties where subdivision and subletting was still extensively practised.[81] However, emigration alone was not the solution to the problems of the estate, but was an important and necessary component. Emigration had to be implemented in conjunction with strict controls over subdivision and the consolidation of holdings into viable farms. It was important that Sir Robert ensured that his estate did not become congested again. Large sums of money were expended in reducing congestion and the last thing he wanted was an influx of paupers on to the estate. As a result of these policies the remaining tenants were able to pay their rents and earn a respectable living from the land.

4. The Gore Booth estate and politics after the Famine

The Gore Booth estate emerged from the tragedy of the Great Famine in a better state than most other Irish properties. While Sir Robert had mortgaged his lands he was not bankrupt and did not have to sell part of his estate in the Encumbered Estates Court as happened with many other landlords. In addition large-scale clearances were not carried out as occurred on many others Irish properties after 1847. A number of reasons contributed to the solvency of the Gore Booth properties. First, he could rely on the income from his Lancashire properties at a time when he was receiving no rents from his Sligo lands. Second, the early 1850s was a period of relative economic prosperity in Ireland with rising agricultural prices fueled by the Crimean War. Tenants were thus able to pay the arrears of rents that had accumulated during the Great Famine years.[1]

As with the rest of the country, the Great Famine resulted in major population change and in the size of holdings in the north Sligo region. By 1852 only 9.2 per cent of the farms in north Sligo were under five acres compared to 12 per cent in 1843, while 25 per cent were over 30 acres compared to 9.2 per cent in 1843. Since the Gore Booth property in north Sligo was scattered over four electoral divisions it is difficult calculate the exact population decline, but Deidre Ryan estimates a 7 per cent decline in the three townlands that Sir Robert owned in the Lissadell East electoral district between 1841 and 1853. The overall population reduction for the division was 26.5 per cent. There was a 7.5 per cent decline on the three Gore Booth townlands in Lissadell West E.D., while the overall reduction was 29 per cent. While Rossinver East E.D., where Sir Robert owned 10 of the 17 townlands, and Carney E.D. where he controlled 8 of the 13 townlands, had population declines of 24 and 26 per cent respectively, much of this was due to Gore Booth's assisted emigration schemes.[2]

Given the level of price increases for agricultural produce in the 1850–76 period, a 40 per cent rise in rents would have been understandable, but the average increase was only 20 per cent.[3] However, major differences existed between estates and even within properties. Rents on the Gore Booth estate for most farms remained unchanged from the early 1840s. By the time of Sir Robert's death in December 1876 they were under the level of Griffith's Valuation which stood at £16,774. The annual rental in the 1870s for the Sligo properties was £15,000.[4] The tenants had virtual fixity of tenure although six tenants were evicted for the non-payment of rent in the 1850s. In October 1851 the *Sligo Champion* reported that tenants had been evicted from the Lissadell part of the property because they owed one year's rent. The agents were blamed, for they had not advised Sir Robert on the matter.[5]

W.E. Vaughan has pointed out that the relationship between landlord, agent and tenants extended beyond that of a simple business association.[6] In some cases, as with Lord Leitrim in Donegal, Sir Roger Palmer in Mayo and William Scully in Ballycohey, Co. Tipperary, this manifested itself in a dictatorial approach: estate rules impinged greatly on the day-to-day lives of the tenants and they lived in constant fear of eviction.[7] However, in other cases the proprietor adopted a more paternalistic role and the tenants' prosperity and well-being was nurtured, as on the Gore Booth estate. Sir Robert's philosophy was that Ireland's prosperity depended largely on the industry of the tenant farmers 'and where industry abounds, prosperity, happiness and independence are sure to follow'.[8] Throughout the decades following the Great Famine, Sir Robert permitted his tenants to dispose of their interest of their holdings, allowing them to secure repayments for improvements.[9] At the same time Gore Booth continued to consolidate the farms when the leases of middlemen expired. In 1874 the lease expired on the townland of Cloonagh, which comprised 300 acres and had a valuation of £159 15s. and a rental of £134. The 43 subtenants were living on small, crowded mud cabins and the land was divided into 560 different plots or fields. One farmer had his holding scattered over 15 places, while another had his seven acres split into 29 divisions. Sir Robert, and his son, Henry, consolidated the holdings into 49 units; new houses and out-buildings were constructed, and new fences and roads put in. The townland of Carrigeens, which covered 289 acres, had a government valuation of £224 15s. and a rental of £212 3s. 7d.; it was squared in the 1870s and improvements carried out. The townland remained congested, with an average farm size of between eight and ten acres. The population depended on fishing for survival. Gore Booth also provided assistance for the farmers on the townland of Doonmore where the farm size ranged from four to six acres. The holdings were not viable and the tenants survived through remittances from friends and relatives in North America, and the sale of turf. Gore Booth helped these tenants supplement their incomes by employing them in the gardens, demesne and the home farm at Lissadell.[10]

In the post-Famine decades most Irish landowners invested little in their estates and this had a detrimental effect on their relationship with their tenants. Vaughan indicates that Irish landlords had a disposable income of about 50 per cent of their total rental income and in general proprietors only spent 11 per cent of their rental on improvements and subscriptions. Although, this varied from property to property, many proprietors spent little on improvements.[11] Half of their rentals were taken up with repayments on encumbrances, taxes, poor law contributions and payments to family members. Out of the disposable income, the upkeep of houses like Lissadell had to be taken care of. In addition if a landowner was an MP, like Gore Booth, there was the added expense of the upkeep of a house in London during the parliamentary season.[12] Sir Robert's London residence was at 7 Buckingham Gardens. He invested heavily in his Sligo property after the Great Famine and in 1863 purchased the townlands of Aughamore, Clogher and Mullaghgar in the barony of Carbury from the earl of Leitrim. His financial position was not helped by the excesses of his brother, Henry, who in 1850 found himself bankrupt with debts of nearly £25,000. Henry's problems were exacerbated by him having to pay maintainance for several illegitimate children that he had fathered through a number of mistresses. He was constantly requesting money from Sir Robert who was prepared to give him partial financial assistance.

The good relations between Sir Robert and his tenants were evident on a number of occasions during the 1850s and 1860s. The tenants openly expressed their gratitude and appreciation towards their proprietor. While it was customary for tenants to make regular affirmations of loyalty to their landlord, this did not mean that all of the people on the estate held the proprietor in high esteem. In some cases the tenants with large holdings organized such presentations and addresses, but the smaller landholders were not always as enthusiastic. The pleas of loyalty on the Gore Booth property were unanimous from all sections of the tenantry and were mainly organized by the local clergy, both Catholic and Protestant, and not by vested interests on the estate. This can be noted in May 1857 when Lady Gore Booth died. The Lissadell tenants met at Castletown schoolhouse and decided to erect a suitable testimonial to express 'the universal feeling of esteem we entertain for her many virtues'. Special mention was made of her charitable work during the Great Famine on behalf of the tenants on the estate. The tenants decided to subscribe towards a memorial window in the new church at Lissadell.[13] Again, in December 1869 the tenants on both the Ballymote and Lissadell properties expressed their gratitude to Sir Robert for the way he dealt with them. The Ballymote address stated 'their sincere feelings of gratitude to you as our landlord, for the excellent manner in which the relations between us are maintained' and the manner in which he 'allowed us many other privileges too numerous to notice in this address.[14] It is also significant that when Gore Booth's role as a landlord was criticized at the 1852 general election, this had been instigated by outsiders with a political agenda which did not take into consideration the good relationship between Sir Robert and his tenants.

The strong bond between landlord and tenant was also displayed in the way the people were prepared to protect Sir Robert's property. The oyster beds in Drumcliff Bay, which covered 55 acres, were a rich source of revenue for the Gore Booth family: the Lissadell oysters, as they were known, had a great reputation in Ireland and Britain, especially London. In November 1864 a series of attacks were made on the beds by dredging by 'pirates' from Coney Island, Rosses Point, Ballinsadare and other coastal areas. After two such incidents the local tenants decided to protect the beds. Night watches were formed and when a group of 'pirates' attempted to take oysters in November 1864 they were forced to retreat by the Gore Booth tenants brandishing scythes, billhooks and blackthorn sticks. Five of the 'pirates' were apprehended and prosecuted.[15]

From the early 1850s Sir Robert held an annual 'Harvest Home' function at Lissadell for the tenants and labourers. Entertainment and food was provided and the guests were waited upon by Sir Robert and other members of the Gore Booth family. The event usually took place in early December when the parliamentary season had ended and was continued on by Sir Robert's son, Henry, when he took over the estate in 1876. This was another indication of the close relationship that existed between the Gore Booths and the tenants.

Throughout his life Gore Booth also developed a close relationship with the wider local community. He was prepared to help with the religious and educational development of the regions that he controlled. He established and paid for a number of schools on his properties such as at Castletown, Milltown and Ballymote. Gore Booth also aided in the building of both Catholic and Church of Ireland churches. By the late 1840s the Catholic chapel in Ballymote was in a poor state with the roof nearly falling in and was too small for the large congregation. In 1848 Sir Robert provided the site free of charge for a new church near the ruins of the old abbey. The foundation stone was not laid until 12 October 1859 because of financial difficulties and was officially opened in September 1864. Gore Booth also subscribed to other local organizations and good causes such as the County Sligo Agricultural Society.

Gore Booth's benevolence and good rapport was observed by the traveller and London *Times* journalist, Finlay Dun, who visited the estate a few years after Sir Robert's death. Dun noted that 'few owners or agents have such intimate knowledge of their tenantry, their holdings or their necessities' and the local population regarded the Gore Booths as their advisers, friends and their arbitrators in the event of family fueds.[17] By 1880 there were 522 tenants on the Lissadell portion of the estate of whom 110 paid less than £4 in rent, 352 between £4 and £20 and 60 paid over £20. There were 454 tenants on the Ballymote property with 112 paying less than £4 in rent (half were town tenants in Ballymote), 262 paid between £4 and £20, and 80 paid more than £20.[18] The total population on the estate was 5,612: 2,827 living at Lissadell and 2,785 at Ballymote.

After his election to parliament as MP for Co. Sligo in 1850 the management of the estate was controlled by Gore Booth's agent, John Gethins.

In 1866 Sir Robert's son, Henry, the father of Eva and Constance Gore Booth, took over the management. This coincided with his father's failing health. Henry was worried about the estate's finances as it remained heavily mortgaged from the relief operations of the Great Famine. Within five years of taking over, the financial position had improved and rents were reduced to the level of Griffith's Valuation.[19]

The 1850s saw the Gore Booth family suffering a number of personal tragedies. In 1852 Sir Robert's brother-in-law, Francis Goold of Dromada, Co. Limerick, died in a boating accident in Sligo Bay, while on holidays at Lissadell. Goold and Sir Robert's eldest son, Robert, got into difficulties at sea and while Robert was saved, Francis drowned.[20] Robert later died in a boating accident in Drumcliff Bay, in which his brother, Henry, was saved. This was followed by the death of Sir Robert's wife, Lady Caroline, in May 1857.

By the 1860s the rest of the family had married. Heney married Georgina Hill of Tickhill Castle, Yorkshire, in 1867. Emily, the eldest daughter, married Captain Charles Wynne, clerk of the peace for Co. Sligo; and Augusta married Owen Wynne, who lived at Hazenwood, Co. Sligo and had an estate of 12,982 acres. These marriage connections were evidence of the high social standing of the Gore Booth family.

Given Gore Booth's important social and political position in Co. Sligo it was inevitable that his name was regularly mentioned as a possible parliamentary candidate. During the 1847 general election it was rumoured that Sir Robert would be one of the Conservative candidates. In July, the *Sligo Journal* reported that Gore Booth was prepared to put his name forward and the newspaper wholeheartedly endorsed his candidacy. He also had the support of the local Catholic clergy, all of the newspapers and the non-electors. The *Champion*, the Repeal newspaper, supported him because no Repeal candidate was contesting the seat and Sir Robert was a resident landowner who had exerted himself for the poor since the commencement of the Famine. The paper was prepared to support any viable candidate as it was totally opposed to the outgoing representatives, Ormsby Gore and John ffolliott.[21] Sir Robert decided not to contest the election. One can only presume that he took the decision because of his commitment to the local relief operations and his unwillingness to get involved in a divisive political contest.

Throughout 1848 and 1849 the *Sligo Champion* was scathing of Ormsby Gore, stating that he was a stranger to the people of Sligo and had done nothing for the poor of Sligo. It continued to champion the campaign to have Sir Robert elected as the next parliamentary representative, but this was done more to undermine the sitting incumbents than outright support for Gore Booth.[22] An opportunity arose in February 1850 when John ffolliott resigned his seat citing ill-health as the reason. The Sligo *Champion* urged Gore Booth to go forward stating:

He is a resident landed proprietor; he spends a large portion of his income at home; the tradesman, the artisan, and the shopkeeper are benefited by him; and he is a politician of moderate views … he has done much good during the years of famine … He did not desert his post, but stood by the people … his kindness to the poor, in the hour of difficulty will not be forgotten, if the hour should come to make it known.[23]

The Dublin *Evening Mail* also strongly supported his candidature stating that Sir Robert was the type of representative that Ireland needed.[24]

Gore Booth was returned unopposed on 12 March 1850, having gained the support of most of the county's landed gentry, all of the local newspapers and the Catholic clergy. He was the only candidate who could have united the county at this point and there was no dissension from the nationalists even though he was standing as a Conservative. It is probable that no other landowner was prepared to contest the election because of their financial difficulties caused by the Famine. The Liberals were also reluctant to fight an election as the Conservatives had a majority of three to one amongst the voters. Sir Robert was proposed by Edward J. Cooper and seconded by Sir William Parke, both landlords in the county. His election address indicated that he certainly was not a radical: he wanted to maintain the connection with Britain and promised to promote the interests of Ireland in every way. He also advocated an extension of the railway to Sligo and the improvement of Sligo harbour.[25]

Sir Robert entered parliament at a time of major political change in Ireland. Within a few months the Russell administration had introduced the Ecclesiastical Titles Bill, which was an attempt to stop the establishment of a Catholic hierarchy in England and Wales. Catholic Ireland was prepared to support their co-religionists in England and Wales and major demonstrations were held throughout Ireland, including one in Sligo on 13 January 1851, at which leading politicians and Catholic churchmen addressed assemblies and passed resolutions condemning the government. Gore Booth attended none of these meetings and issued no statement of support. At no time did he offer any opinion on the subject and it would appear that he was adopting the approach that he pursued with the Famine operations: staying out of the limelight and keeping a low profile. As the Ecclesiastical Titles Bill was such an emotive issue for Irish Catholics this was the wrong option.

By this time the Irish electorate had increased significantly because of the Irish Franchise Act of 1850 which extended the vote to tenants with holdings valued at or over £12. As a result the number of electors rose from 45,000 to 132,245. The impact on Co. Sligo was significant with the electorate increasing from 837 in 1847 to 2,105 in 1852. As the act mainly benefited middle-class tenant farmers who were closely allied to the Catholic clergy, this new force proved a major threat to the landlords' electoral power. All landowners, regardless of how they treated their tenants in the past, were now regarded as the political enemy. This new force was mobilized into the Tenant Right movement and held demonstrations throughout the country with local branches being established in most counties. Once again Sir Robert refused to associate himself with this new organization.

Sir Robert's failure to espouse these popular causes quickly alienated a section of the Sligo population and by the autumn of 1851 he was being severely criticized by nationalist and Liberal groups because of his parliamentary voting record, in particular on issues associated with land and religion. Much of the opposition was being orchestrated by the *Sligo Champion* which said that the county would not benefit with Gore Booth as its representative, describing him as being 'of the silver fork school and the homely farmer is dirt in their nostril'. Although he was impressive at home, in the wider political world he was unable to cope with the intellectual giants in parliament.[26]

It was this negativity which set the tone for the general election contest in 1852 when Gore Booth's activities during the Famine and his actions as a landlord were questioned and became major issues in the campaign. The attacks originated from the County Sligo Independent Club which was established on 18 March 1852 and was controlled by the bishop of Elphin and the local Catholic clergy. Its aim was to have two Liberal representatives elected for the county at the general election. It was decided at a meeting of the club on 24 April to select Richard Swift, the Catholic sheriff of London, and John Ball as the Liberal candidates.[27] The club was confident that the Liberals would win a seat for the first time since 1800 as there was now a majority of Catholic voters in the constituency – 1,162 Catholic voters against 632 Protestants, with 270 having died or emigrated.[28]

Sir Robert found that the political climate had changed and he was fighting a contest where not only his politics were being condemned, but also his reputation as a landlord and his personal integrity were being questioned. It was alleged that he was an exterminator who had razed 2,350 houses during the recent Famine and that the Lissadell tenants had died in their thousands in ditches like vermin or in watery graves. It was also stated that he had deliberately sent out his tenants to North America in 1839 on the *Pomona* which had sank and all the passengers had drowned. This was the first time that this allegation was publicly made. What was even more disconcerting was that the charges came from local Catholic clergymen like Fr Noone of Ahamlish and Fr Patrick O'Gara of Drumcliff who had publicly defended Gore Booth's reputation in the past and who had worked with him on local relief committees during the Famine. During the campaign it was also claimed that Gore Booth had opposed all legislation relating to tenant right and land legislation. Sir Robert refuted these statements and said that he would support any measure which 'without infringing on the rights of property, will secure to the tenant the full and fair value of the outlay of his capital on the improvement of the soil'.[29]

The question has to be asked why did Fr O'Gara and the Catholic clergy become so vociferous in their opposition to Sir Robert's candidature and orchestrate the personal attacks, especially having defended him so stoutly in 1847? The Conservative newspaper, the *Sligo Chronicle* and the *Sligo Journal*, published O'Gara's letter dated 6 February 1847 when he wrote to Lady Gore Booth complementing her on the way that she and her husband had looked after the poor and allowing 'that the destitute poor are permitted to use the broth etc, every day during Lent'. He added that their exertions entitled them 'to the eternal gratitude of every friend of suffering humanity, as well as of the freedom of conscience' and that the people prayed every night for Lady Caroline's family.[30] Sir Robert was extremely unhappy with the clergy's personal attacks on him. In his 1852 election address he said 'I had hoped that my past conduct among you, during a period of more than ordinary trial (to which, from personal motives, I wish not further to allude), would have been a sufficient protection against such slander, got up by interested and designing parties and with no other object than to render me unpopular'.[31] This was the only occasion throughout his political career that Gore Booth made any reference to his role during the Great Famine. He had been forced into making this statement because of the personal and vindictive attacks that were orchestrated against him. Both the *Sligo Journal* and *Sligo Chronicle* defended him. The *Chronicle* said that the conduct of the priests had surprized everyone, while the *Journal* stated that the clergy were 'using all their influence to turn the sectarian animosity of an ignorant and ungrateful people' against Sir Robert.[32]

While a number of recent studies have alluded to the attacks by O'Gara and Noone during the election campaign, none have attempted to offer any explanation. The early 1850s was a period of reinterpretation and reevalu-ation of the landlords' role during the Great Famine and the image of the exterminator and ruthless proprietors gained credence. The motives of those landowners who were involved in relief operations were questioned and their good deeds eroded from the folk memory, as landowners were depicted as people who did nothing to save their tenants. The work of the marquis of Sligo, George Henry Moore, Major Charles O'Hara of Annaghmore, Sir Robert Gore Booth and others were quickly forgotten during the clear-ances and evictions of the 1850s. In the rush to demonize landlords in general, the work of individual charitable landowners was quickly forgotten. At the same time the County Sligo Independent Club made it clear that it wanted to have power over their representatives and wanted candidates who advocated tenant right, changes in the poor law and the abrogation of enactments against civil and religious liberties. Thus Gore Booth was being condemned and opposed because he was standing as a Conservative. As the Conservatives had been the dominant political force in Co. Sligo since 1800 this was the first realistic opportunity that the Liberals had of taking a seat. It was maintained that the Catholic clergy would ensure that the voters elected Liberal candidates, implying that every method would be used to defeat the Conservative candidates.[33] During the campaign Richard Swift had the open support of the local Catholic priests who accompanied him to most of the meetings. Swift also had the support of Archbishop John MacHale of Tuam because he was prepared to 'aid us in protecting our religion from penalties and our people from utter ruin'.[34]

While it appeared that Sir Robert was facing major electoral difficulties he was assisted by the rumour that he had the support of Lord Palmerston, himself a Whig member of parliament, who was reputed to have told his Co. Sligo agent, Edward Smith, that his tenants should vote for Gore Booth.[35] As will be seen later, Palmerston was not prepared to instruct his tenants as to how they should vote in the election, but there is no doubt that the rumour resulted in some tenants supporting Sir Robert. These tenants were also prepared to support Sir Robert because of the relief he provided during the Famine.

Compared to other constituencies where there was widespread voter intimidation and violence, the Co. Sligo election passed off relatively peacefully. Sir Robert headed the poll with 943 votes and Swift took the second seat with 870 votes. Many Catholics voted for Gore Booth or split their vote when they could easily have 'plumped' for the Liberal candidate. There were post-election allegations of widespread voter intimidation, but these were never proven.[36] In late 1852 it was claimed that Sir Robert's agents were responsible for the illegal treating of voters in Ballymote and Easkey during the contest and that they issued receipts for rents on condition that the tenants voted for Sir Robert. Parliament was unsuccessfully petitioned to overturn the election result.[37] It would appear that the action was designed to counteract a petition initiated by the Conservatives to overturn the result of the Sligo borough election.

Sir Robert Gore Booth served as the MP for Co. Sligo for twenty-six years, but of the seven elections that he fought the 1852 contest was by far the most difficult and bruising. His electoral success was largely due to his popularity within the county and an ability to survive the changing political moods, feelings and atmosphere that was part of the Irish political landscape in the decades following the Great Famine. In the 1850s he had to survive the swing to the Irish Independent Party, in 1868 the overwhelming support for Gladstone and Church Disestablishment and in 1874 the rising tide that was the Home Rule movement. He was returned unopposed on four occasions and the only time his seat was severely threatened was in 1868 when he secured the second seat against his Conservative running mate, Lt

Col. E.H. O'Connor. His political survival can be attributed to the esteem in which he was held by the general Sligo population and electorate. Even the Catholic clergy came to tolerate him although his parliamentary actions were not always welcomed. While they regarded him as a benevolent and generous landowner there were occasions when Sir Robert was reprimanded and censured. In July 1865 Bishop Laurence Gillooly of Elphin gave him a stern lecture because he had voted against the Catholic Church's wishes on Mr Monsell's County Oaths bill and 'previously on several divisions affecting the liberty of our Church'. Gillooly added that 'those votes are incompatible with the admission of your claims to civil and religious equality', but he stressed that Sir Robert was 'a kind and generous proprietor'. Gore Booth was elected unopposed at the subsequent general election as Gillooly was not prepared to support any other candidate.[38]

Gore Booth's electoral survival as a Conservative was also aided by the disorganization of the Liberal Party within Sligo throughout most of the 1850s and 1860s. The County Sligo Independent Club declined quickly after the 1852 election because of divisions between the Liberals and the local clergy. At the 1859 general election the Liberals withdrew the candidature of Henry J. Lynch because Dr Gillooly and the priests refused to support him.[39] The failure to contest the election was surprising since there was an 800 Catholic majority in the county and one of the principal landowners in the country, Lord Palmerston, a Whig was prime minister in the late 1850s. At no point did he or his representatives in Sligo make any attempt to further the Liberal cause in the county. Various moves were made in the 1850s and 1860s to establish a Liberal club in Sligo, as in July 1859, but these attempts failed largely because of clerical indifference and at times hostility. During the 1857 contest some of the leading priests in the county, such as Owen Feeney, Patrick O'Gara and Patrick Conway refused to support the Liberal candidates, Richard Swift and John Ball, and indicated that they were voting for Sir Robert.[40] Such divisions in the Liberal ranks worked to Gore Booth's advantage.

Despite his relatively safe parliamentary seat, there were occasions when Sir Robert was worried for his political survival. The threats in 1852 and 1868 were not because of his role as a landowner, but because of the rise of nationalist issues and the intervention of the Catholic clergy. Sir Robert was aware that the clergy were a major political broker in the county and their intervention in supporting his Liberal opponents threatened his parliamentary career. In January 1868 Gore Booth did not endear himself to the Catholic clergy and Bishop Gillooly by absenting himself from a meeting of the clergy and the people of the diocese of Elphin in Roscommon called to support Gladstone's Disestablishment of the Church of Ireland bill. In the following weeks, contributors to the *Sligo Champion* asked whether there was no suitable Catholic candidate available to represent the county.[41] A further meeting of the Liberal electors was held on 9 July and Gillooly in proposing the first resolution, stated that Gore Booth did not represent the majority of the electors of Sligo and nominated the Catholic, Denis M. O'Conor, a brother of the O'Conor Don, Catholic MP for Co. Roscommon, to contest the county for the Liberal party. [42] Sir Robert had every reason to be worried as the priests became an important part of O'Conor's election team: ten priests were present when the Liberal candidate addressed a demonstration in Tubbercurry on 7 September, seven at Easkey on 7 October, eight at Riverstown on 25 October and eleven at Grange on 2 November. The clergy's involvement in 1852 and 1868 was probably the reason why Gore Booth approached the other major political power brokers in Sligo, the landlords, looking for their support. However he did not always get the response he hoped for. Lord Palmerston in 1852 and Lady Palmerston in 1868, while acknowledging Sir Robert's suitability for office, were adamant that they would not pressurize their tenants into voting for him, or indeed for any other candidate. Lady Palmerston went even further and stated that as the family were Liberals, she would find it difficult to support Sir Robert's candidature. [43]

While Sir Robert was a parliamentary representative for Co. Sligo for over twenty-six years his attendance in the house of commons was infrequent and his contribution to parliamentary debate largely uneventful. Some groups in Sligo were highly critical of his parliamentary performance. The *Sligo Champion* frequently ridiculed his actions in the house of commons stating that his past endeavours indicated that he was perfectly indifferent to the local mercantile interests in Sligo and had done nothing to improve Sligo harbour or railway communications to the county. [44] Despite this lacklustre parliamentary career the county electorate continued to keep faith in him, a further indication of how well he was regarded by the local population.

Gore Booth usually took up residence in London for the parliamentary session in February after the annual horse fair at Catnagat near Collooney. A number of servants from Lissadell and the rest of the Gore Booth family followed him later. The servants that went to 7 Buckingham Gate included the first and second housemaids, the house steward, the groom chambers, the under butler, and first and second footman. The rest of the Lissadell staff remained in Sligo to look after the house until the family's return at the end of the parliamentary session. [45]

By late 1875 Gore Booth was in poor health, suffering from severe gout, and, on doctors' advice, did not attend the 1876 parliamentary season at Westminster. His death on 21 December 1876 came as a surprise as he appeared to be in reasonable health in the previous weeks and had attended the annual 'Harvest Home' celebration for the tenants at Lissadell. The family suffered a double tragedy as his niece, Isabella McCool Gore Booth, who was visiting Lissadell, died three days later. The two bodies were buried together in the family vault in St John's churchyard, Sligo. A large group of the Lissadell tenants walked behind the hearse from Lissadell to Sligo. Most of the local gentry attended, including the O'Conor Don, MP, the earl of Leitrim, earl of Kingston, Lord Cole, Captain King-Harman, Lord Harlech and Lieutenant-Colonel ffolliott. Bishop Laurence Gillooly of Elphin and three parish priests were also present. The *Sligo Champion*, the newspaper which had been so critical of him in the 1850s, best summed up his qualities.

> In every position in life Sir Robert displayed the highest principles of integrity and humanity. Although he was conservative in his politics and strongly attached to the religion he belonged to, he never allowed his religion or his politics to interfere in his dealings with his tenantry, employers, etc.[46]

Conclusion

Sir Robert Gore Booth's role in history has been largely neglected by historians. Despite the availability of his papers and those of the Lissadell estate in the Public Record Office of Northern Ireland and the publication of his evidence to a number of parliamentary select committees and commissions, his role as a landlord and his relationship with his tenants has been largely ignored or confined to the margins of history. This is in sharp contrast to the renown of Lissadell House, immortalized by William Butler Yeats as having inspired his poetry, or with Sir Robert's granddaughter, Constance Gore Booth (Constance Markievicz), whose life as a revolutionary, politician and champion of the rights of the working classes and of women, has been studied in numerous works by academics and scholars.

Sir Robert's omission from Irish history must be understood in the context of how Irish landlords as a group have been assessed and portrayed. The intolerance and excesses of many proprietors towards their tenants have been used to demonize nearly all landowners, and the progressive and charitable efforts of a few, including Gore Booth, have been ignored or brushed out of history. Like most landowners, Sir Robert saw land as an economic resource which had to be worked to its ultimate to produce a maximum return. However, he differed from most other landowners in that he was more compassionate and considerate towards the tiller of the soil. Gore Booth was adamant that farms had to be viable, otherwise the tenants would remain poor and constantly face famine. For this reason holdings on his estate were consolidated into economic units, rundale ended and capital provided to improve the land and the estate's infrastructure.

Gore Booth's attitude towards his tenants and the wider community can be observed during the Great Famine: he not only spent a large sum of money providing relief works on his estate and purchasing food, but much of his time was devoted to working on relief committees, distributing aid and bringing journalists and officials to witness the horrors and devastation that accompanied the potato failure in north Sligo. This was at a time when the entire landlord community in Ireland was being attacked and condemned for their inactivity and insensitivity towards their tenants by the government, nationalists and Catholic clergy. While the philanthropic deeds of a small number of landowners, such as Gore Booth did little in the overall alleviation of hunger and destitution, their role in helping their people survive should be acknowledged. Sir Robert saw assisted emigration to

North America of his surplus tenants as the solution to congestion, especially during the Great Famine. While initially this was estate driven, during the late 1840s the tenants viewed emigration as a way of escape and beseeched the landlord to facilitate their passage. Unlike many other landlord assisted emigration plans, the Gore Booth schemes were well organized and reasonably well resourced, and the landlord was actively involved in the process at all times. While some of his former tenants encountered problems after their arrival in North America, Sir Robert cannot be entirely blamed for their difficulties.

While questions were asked regarding the merits of the emigration schemes and the motivation of those landlords who implemented them on their properties, it must be noted that while some proprietors saw them as a way of clearing their estates, others regarded such schemes as an opportunity for the tenants to start a new life in a new country. The alternative was a continuation of poverty and destitution, and during the Great Famine probable death. At best it would mean an uncertain future in the workhouse. Gore Booth's emigration schemes can thus be seen as providing a fresh start for his tenants and under the circumstances he contributed as much as he possibly could towards their exodus and passage to British North America.

Gore Booth had a long parliamentary career and this coincided with a period of major change in Irish politics. The post-Famine decades saw the demise of the landlords' political authority as their power came under threat from issues such as tenant right, church disestablishment and home rule. It was a period of uncertainty which saw the erosion of this power. Gore Booth, like many other Irish proprietors who went to Westminster, had a largely uneventful parliamentary career and Hansard shows that he contributed little to the parliamentary debates in his twenty-six years in the house of commons. He displayed a certain arrogance and contempt for his constituents as he represented the interests of the landed classes and not those of all of his constituents. This can be seen in his lack of support, or at best ambivalence, towards tenant right or issues which affected the Catholic Church in Ireland. Sir Robert's ability to survive as the MP for Co. Sligo for such a long period must be attributed to the failure of local nationalists, Liberals and the Catholic clergy to provide a united, long-term political alternative to landlord control. This situation was not unique to Sligo and was repeated in many other Irish counties. Landowners were worried by this threat to their political authority as can be noted by Sir Robert's concerns during the 1852 and 1868 contests.

Sir Robert Gore Booth died in December 1876, just before the major changes that transformed landlord-tenant relations occurred: the formation of the Land League in 1879 and the introduction of the 1881 Land Act which legalized the 3Fs – fixity of tenure, free sale and fair rent. In December 1876 few people could have envisaged the imminent demise of the social, political and economic influence of the Irish landlord. While the agrarian revolution of 1879–82 changed the relationship between landlord and tenant, it must be emphasized that it had little impact on the situation on the Gore Booth estate where the good relations and paternalism that existed between Sir Robert and his tenants were continued by his son, Sir Henry. His death also occurred just before the decline of the landlords' political power as was evident in the 1880 general election which saw the emergence of Charles Stewart Parnell as a major political force in the country, opening the way for a new political influence that was largely at the expense of the Irish landowners.

Notes

ABBREVIATIONS

CSORP   Chief Secretary's Office, Registered Papers
Devon Commission   *Evidence taken before her majesty's commissioners of inquiry into the*
                    state of the law and practice in respect to the occupation of land in
                    Ireland, HC 1845 (605), XIX
HC   House of Commons
IHS   *Irish Historical Studies*
MT   *Mayo Telegraph*
NAI   National Archives of Ireland
PRONI   Public Record Office of Northern Ireland
SC   *Sligo Champion*
SJ   *Sligo Journal*

INTRODUCTION

1 See W.E.Vaughan, *Landlords and tenants in mid-Victorian Ireland* (Oxford, 1994); Gerard Moran, 'Landlord and tenant relations in Ireland: Sir Arthur Guinness and his estate at Ashford Castle, 1868–1882', *Cathair na Mart*, 10 (1990), 69–78.
2 Liam Dolan, *The third earl of Leitrim* (Fanad, 1978).
3 See Christine Kinealy, *This great calamity: the Irish Famine, 1845–52* (Dublin, 1994); James S. Donnelly, *The Great Irish Potato Famine* (Stroud, 2002).
4 See Gerard Moran, *Sending out Ireland's poor: assisted emigration to North America in the 19th century* (Dublin, 2004), ch. 2.
5 See Donald J. Jordan, 'John O'Connor Power, Charles Stewart Parnell and the centralization of popular politics in Ireland', *IHS*, 25 (1986), 46–66; K. Theodore Hoppen, *Elections, politics and Society in Ireland, 1832–1885* (Oxford, 1984), ch. vi; Gerard Moran, 'Philip Callan: the rise and fall of an Irish nationalist MP, 1868–1886', *County Louth Archeological and Historical Journal,* 22:4 (1992), 395–411.

1. THE GORE BOOTHS AND THEIR ESTATE BEFORE THE FAMINE

1 PRONI, Lissadell papers D/4131; Diana Norman, *Terrible beauty: a life of Constance Markievicz* (London, 1987), pp 17–18; Joe McGowan, (ed.), *Constance Markievicz; the people's countess* (Mullaghmore, 2003), p. 56.
2 PRONI, Lissadell papers D/4131; Henry Heaney, (ed.), *A Scottish Whig in Ireland, 1835–1838: the journals of Robert Graham of Redgorton* (Dublin, 1999), p. 339.
3 PRONI, Lissadell papers, D/4131; Settlement of the second marriage of Sir Robert Gore Booth to Caroline Goold, dated 1 Apr. 1830 (PRONI, Gore Booth papers, D/4051/5) Heaney, *Scottish Whig in Ireland,* p. 23 n. 15.
4 Dermot James, *The Gore Booths of Lissadell* (Dublin, 2004), p. 13.
5 Ibid., p.12.
6 Marianne Heron, *The hidden houses of Ireland* (Dublin, 1999), pp 79–80. PRONI, Lissadell papers, D/4131.
7 PRONI, Lissadell papers, D/4131/H/3.
8 John Mc Ternan, *Olde Sligo: aspects of town and county over 750 years* (Sligo, 1995), p. 294.

9 Reminiscences of Sam Waters, 1846–1922 (PRONI, Gore Booth papers, D/4051/14).

10 Ibid.

11 James, *Gore Booths of Lissadell*, p. 50.

12 See Gerard Moran, 'Absentee landlordism in Mayo in the 1870s', *Cathair na Mart*, 2 (1982), 30–4; N.D. Palmer, 'Irish absenteeism in the 1870s', *Journal of Modern History*, 12 (1940).

13 Andrew Motherwell to Gore Booth, 12 July 1820 (PRONI, Lissadell papers, D/4231/H/16).

14 William Goddart to George Dodwell, 3 Nov. 1823 in ibid.

15 Henry Coulter, *The West of Ireland: its existing condition and prospects* (Dublin, 1862), pp 280–2.

16 *Devon commission*, pt ii, pp 204–5, qs 37–40.

17 George Dodwell's account with Robert Gore Booth for four years rent of the Ballymote estate from the commencement to 1 May 1837 (PRONI, Lissadell papers, D/4131/H/4).

18 Robert Lyons to Sir Robert Newcome Gore Booth, 25 Mar. 1810 (PRONI, Lissadell papers D/4131/H/16).

19 *Second report of the select committee of the House of Lords on colonization from Ireland*, HC 1847–8 (593), xvii, p. 255, q. 2599.

20 Deirdre Ryan, 'The Lissadell estate of Sir Robert Gore Booth: famine and emigration, 1845–47' (unpublished MA thesis, UCD, 1996), pp 1–2.

21 *Second report of the select committee on colonization from Ireland*, p. 270, q. 2725.

22 Richard Getting to Vernon, dated 1847 (PRONI, Lissadell papers, D/4131/H/8); *Second report of the select committee on colonization*, p. 269, q. 2725.

23 Heaney, *Scottish Whig in Ireland*, pp 344–5.

24 *Second report of the select committee on colonization*, p. 258, q. 2628.

25 *Devon commission* , pt I, HC 1845 (605), xix, p. 31, q. 29; p. 32 q. 55; pt ii, (616), xx, p.203, q. 20.

26 Daniel Grace, *The Great Famine in Nenagh poor law union, Co. Tipperary* (Nenagh, 2000), pp 8–9.

27 See evidence of R.S. Guinness, *Devon commission*, pt 1, p. 47, q. 220–3.

28 ibid., p. 31 q. 20.

28 See Patrick J. Duffy, 'Management problems on a large estate in mid-19th-century Ireland: William Steuart Trench's report on the Shirley estate in 1843', *Clogher Record*, 16:1 (1997), 101.

30 *Devon commission*, pt 1, p. 204, q. 70; p. 205, q. 45.

31 *Second report of the select committee on colonization*, p. 272, q. 2765–6.

32 *Devon commission*, pt ii, p. 203, q. 5–6.

33 Ryan, 'Lissadell estate of Sir Robert Gore Booth', p. 7.

34 *Second report of the select committee on colonization*, p. 258, q. 2636–8.

35 Samuel Lewis, *Topographical dictonary of Ireland*, (1837), i, p. 513.

36 *Devon commission*, pt ii, supplement pt 2, pp 87–8.

37 Names of Ballygilgan tenants who got land elsewhere (PRONI, Lissadell papers, D/4131/H/8).

38 Account for Ballygilgan tenants for 1830–41, 6 Nov. 1844 in ibid.

39 See Finlay Dun, *Landlords and tenants in Ireland* (London, 1881), p. 194.

40 *Devon commission*, pt ii, pp 203–4, qs 21, 26, 35; Dun, *Landlords and tenants*, p. 195; PRONI, Lissadell papers, D/4131, appendix A; James, *Gore Booths of Lissadell*, pp 27–8.

41 Coulter, *The West of Ireland*, pp 280–2.

42 *Devon commission*, pt i, p. 32, qs 52–3.

43 *Second report of the select committee on colonization*, p. 259, q. 2639.

44 Joe McGowan, *Echoes of a strange land* (Cork and Dublin, 2001), pp 184–5.

45 Dun, *Landlords and tenants*, p 192–3; Extract from the journal kept by Perton Hart (one of the commissioners appointed to enquire into the condition of the poorer classes in Ireland, Aug.–Sept. 1833 (PRONI, Lissadell papers, D/4131/H/15).

46 Journal of Perton Hart (PRONI, Lissadell papers, D/4131/H/15).

47 *Report from the select committee of the House of Lords on colonization from Ireland*, HC 1847–8 (418), xvii, q 2631–2.

48 *Second report of the select committee on colonization*, p. 268, q. 2708–12.

49 Proposal of a sinking fund by Thomas Goold to Sir Robert Gore Booth, 21 Mar. 1833 (PRONI, Lissadell papers, D/4131/H/4); *Devon commissions*, pt 1, p. 35, q. 107.
50 PRONI, Lissadell papers, D/4231.
51 Ibid.
52 Charles Townley to Sir Robert Gore Booth, 28 Mar. 1848 (PRONI, Lissadell papers, D/4231/H/1)
53 Andrew Motherwell to Gore Booth, 12 Jul. 1820 (PRONI, Lissadell papers, D4231/H/16.
54 George Dodwell's account with Robert Gore Booth for four years rent of the Ballymote estate from the commencement to 1 May 1837 (PRONI, Lissadell papers, D/4131/H/4).
55 Rentals for Lissadell for 1843 (PRONI, Lissadell papers, D/4131/H/8).
56 Ryan, 'Lissadell estate of Sir Robert Gore Booth', p. 9.
57 *Devon commission*, pt ii, p. 222, q. 17–8.
58 James, *Gore Booths of Lissadell*, pp 24–5.
59 Letter from M.H. Slade to Constable ?, 28 Sept. 1842 (PRONI, Lissadell papers, D/4131/H/6).
60 Address to Sir Robert Gore Booth by his Carney tenants, 5 Oct. 1845 (PRONI, Lissadell papers, D/4131/H9).

2. SIR ROBERT GORE BOOTH AND THE GREAT FAMINE IN NORTH SLIGO

1 Sub-Inspector, Ballymote to Col. Duncan MacGregor, 22 Sept. 1845 (NAI, Famine Commission papers, RLFC, 2/213120).
2 Mc Tiernan, *Olde Sligo*, p. 311.
3 Mary Daly, *The Famine in Ireland* (Dublin, 1986), p. 39.
4 *MT*, 24 Dec. 1845.
5 John Scott to the Relief Committee, 28 Apr. 1846 (NAI, Famine Relief Committee, Sligo, RLFC, 3/1/1901).
6 *MT*, 6 May 1846.
7 *Correspondence from July 1846 to January 1847, relating to measures adopted for the relief of distress in Ireland*, HC 1847 (761), li, p. 57.
8 Helen Hatton, *The largest amount of Good: Quaker relief in Ireland, 1654–1921* (Kingston & Montreal, 1993), p. 83.
9 *SC*, 1 Aug. 1846.
10 Resolution of the Corran Relief Committee, dated 21 Aug. 1846 (NAI, CSORP, Distress papers, DP 4407).
11 Thomas Power, 'The Palmerston estate in County Sligo: improvement and assisted emigration before 1850' in Patrick J. Duffy (ed), *To and from Ireland: planned migration schemes, c. 1600–2000* (Dublin, 2004), pp 118–9.
12 Liam Swords, *A dominant church: the diocese of Achonry, 1818–1960* (Dublin, 2004), pp 146–7.
13 Revd J. Garrett to William Stanley, 23 Oct. 1846 (NAI, Famine Relief Commission papers, RLFC 3/2/26/18).
14 *SC*, 31 Oct. 1846; *TH*, 5 Nov. 1856.
15 *Second report of the select committee on colonization from Ireland*, p. 255, q. 2604.
16 *SJ*, 17 Dec. 1847.
17 Ibid., 19 Mar. 1847; 27 Apr. 1848.
18 *Distress in Ireland, supplementary appendix to the seventh report from the relief commission*, HC 1847–8, xxix, p. 80.
19 *SJ*, 29 Oct. 1847.
20 Report from Capt. Gilbert on Sligo workhouse, 24 Nov. 1847 (NAI, CSORP, 1847/012196; *SJ*, 10 Dec. 1847.
21 James S. Donnelly, Jr, 'Landlords and tenants' in W.E. Vaughan, (ed.), *A new history of Ireland, V: Ireland under the union, I, 1801–1870* (Oxford, 1989), p. 336.
22 Ryan, 'Lissadell estate of Gore Booth', p. 13.
23 Resolution of a meeting of the landed proprietors and cesspayers in Sligo, 23 Dec. 1846 (NAI, CSORP, 0342); *SJ*, 1 Jan. 1847.
24 See Moran, *Sending out Ireland's poor*, pp 49–50.
25 James H. Tuke, *A visit to Connaught in the autumn of 1847* (London, 1848), p. 15.
26 Liam Swords, *In their own words: the Famine in north Connacht, 1845–49* (Dublin, 1999), p. 284.

27 Ryan, 'Lissadell estate of Gore Booth', p. 13.
28 Swords, *In their own words*, pp 437–9.
29 *SC*, 19 Dec. 1846.
30 *SJ*, 26 Feb. 1846.
31 *SC*, 13 Feb. 1847.
32 Swords, *A dominant church*, p.1, 44.
33 Revd J. Garrell to William Stanley, 4 Feb. 1847 (NAI, Famine Relief Commission papers, RLFC, 3/2/26/18).
34 Minutes of the meetings of the Famine Relief Committee (PRONI, Lissadell papers, D/4131/H/15).
35 Revd J. Garrell to William Stanley, 4 Feb. 1847 (NAI, Famine Relief Commission papers, RLFC, 3/2/26/18).
36 *Second report of the select committee on colonization*, pp 235–6.
37 Ibid., pp 262, 268.
38 Ryan, 'Lissadell estate of Gore Booth', p. 20.
39 *Second report of the select committee on colonization*, pp 276–81.
40 Swords, *In their own words*, p. 148; *SJ*, 10 Dec. 1847.
41 Swords, *A dominant church*, pp 153; *SJ*, 19 Feb. 1848.
42 *Correspondence from January to March 1847, relating to measures adopted for the relief of distress in Ireland* (Board of Works series, second part), HC 1847 (797), lii, p. 180.
43 Ibid., p. 263.
44 Letter from ? to Sir Robert Gore Booth, 13 Jan. 1847 (PRONI, Lissadell papers, D/4131/H/8).
45 *Correspondence from January to March 1847, relating to measures adopted for the relief of distress in Ireland*, p. 183; James, *Gore Booths of Lissadell*, pp 30–1.
46 Ryan, 'Lissadell estate of Gore Booth', pp 24–5; *SJ*, 15 Oct. 1847.
47 Ryan, 'Lissadell estate of Gore Booth', p. 25; Power, 'Palmerston estate in County Sligo', p. 120.
48 Ryan, 'Lissadell estate of Gore Booth', p. 26.
49 Ibid., p. 17.
50 *SJ*, 15 Jul. 1847.
51 *SC*, 2 Jan.; 16 Jun. 1847.
52 Ibid., 30 Jan.; 20 Feb.; 13 Mar. 1847.
53 Letter from Sir Robert Gore Booth

undated 1847 (PRONI, Lissadell papers, D/4131/H/8); James, *Gore Booths of Lissadell*, p. 34.
54 Swords, *In their own words*, pp 147–8; Cormac Ó Grada, *Black 47 and beyond: the great Irish Famine in history, economy and memory* (Princeton, 1999), p. 64.
55 Ryan, 'Lissadell estate of Gore Booth', p. 14.
56 *SC*, 2 Oct.; 23 Oct. 1847.
57 See *SJ*, 21 Apr.; 12 May 1848.
58 Dun, *Landlords and tenants*, p. 191.
59 *Second report of the select committee on colonization*, p. 255, q. 2598.
60 Letter from Sir Robert Gore Booth, undated 1847 (PRONI, Lissadell papers, D/4131/H/8).
61 McGowan, *Constance Markievicz*, p. 57; Tyler Anbinder, 'Lord Palmerston and the Irish Famine emigration', *Historical Journal*, 44: 2 (2001), p. 451.
62 *Second report of the select committee on colonization*, p. 282.
63 *Correspondence from January to March 1847, relating to measures adopted for the relief of distress in Ireland* (Commissariat series, second part), HC 1847 (796), lii, p. 196.
64 Reprinted in *MT*, 16 Sept. 1846.
65 Christine Kinealy, *This great calamity: the Irish Famine, 1845–52* (Dublin, 1994), pp 51–2.
66 *SC*, 27 Mar. 1847.
67 Ó Gráda, *Black '47 and beyond*, pp 128–9.
68 See *SC*, 3 Apr. 1847.
69 Ibid., 25 Sept. 1846; *Nation*, 3 Oct. 1846.
70 Fr Patrick O'Gara to Sir Robert Gore Booth, March 1848 (PRONI, Lissadell papers, D/4131/H/8).
71 *SJ*, 10 Dec. 1847.
72 Letter from Sir Robert Gore Booth, undated 1847 (PRONI, Lissadell papers, D/4131/H/8)

3. THE ASSISTED EMIGRATION SCHEMES

1 See Moran, *Sending out Ireland's poor*, pp 29–31.
2 *Minutes of evidence before the select committee on the employment of the poor in Ireland*, HC 1823 (561), vi, p. 190.

3 Evidence of Joseph Kincaid in *Minutes
of evidence of the select committee of the
House of Lords on colonization from
Ireland*, HC 1847 (737), p. 160, q. 1552.
4 Devon commission, pt ii, HC 1845
(616), xx, p. 205, q. 51.
5 *Second report of the select committee on
colonization*, p. 259, q. 2641.
6 Devon commission, pt ii, supplement,
pt 2, p. 88, q. 15; *Second report of select
committee on colonization*, p. 259, q. 2639;
see also, p. 270, qs 2726–9.
7 An account of money given by Sir
Robert Gore Booth, bart, to the
Ballygilgan tenants for taking down
their houses and potato trak at the rate
of £4 per acre (PRONI, Lissadell
papers, D/4131/H/8).
8 Moran, *Sending out Ireland's poor*,
pp 48–9.
9 *Minutes of evidence of select committee on
colonization*, p. 158, q. 1531. See also
David Fitzpatrick, 'Emigration,
1801–70' in Vaughan (ed.), *A new
history of Ireland*, v, p. 589.
10 *Second report of the select committee of the
house of lords on colonization from Ireland*,
p. 266; see also Tyler Anbinder, *Five
Points: the 19th century New York City
neighbourhood that invented tap dance,
stole elections and became the world's
most notorious slum* (New York, 2001),
p. 61.
11 Passengers of the *Lady Sale*, July 1847
(PRONI, Lissadell Papers,
D/4131/H/8).
12 Account of expenses attending the
emigration from Ballygilgan (PRONI,
Lissadell papers, D/4131/H/8).
13 Evidence of T.W.C Murdock, *Second
report of the select on colonization from
Ireland*, p. 294, q. 2866.
14 *Minutes of evidence from the third report
before the select committee on emigration
from the United Kingdom*, 1827, HC
1826–7 (550), v, p. 451, q. 4336.
15 *Report from the select committee on
colonization from Ireland*, p. 260 q. 2642.
16 *Second report of the select committee on
colonization from Ireland*, pp 259–60, q.
2643. See also copy of letter from Sir
Robert Gore Booth, 16 March 1848
(PRONI, Lissadell papers,
D/4131/H8).

17 *Second report of the select committee on
colonization from Ireland*, p. 275, q. 2786;
Patrick O'Gara to Sir Robert Gore
Booth, 21 Mar. 1848 (PRONI.
Lissadell papers, D/4131/H/8); Terry
Coleman, *Passage to America: from Great
Britain and Ireland to America in the mid-
19th century* (London, 1972), p. 202
18 *Second report of the select committee on
colonization from Ireland*, pp 261–2,
q. 2655.
19 Moran, *Sending out Ireland poor*,
pp 51–3.
20 *Second report of the select committee of the
House of Lords on colonization from
Ireland*, p. 262, q. 2668.
21 Ibid., pp 262–3, q. 2668, p. 281; Donald
MacKay, *Flight from Famine: the coming
of the Irish to Canada* (Toronto, 1990),
p. 282.
22 See letter of John Purden to Henry
Gore Booth in *Third report of the select
committee of the house of lords on
colonization from Ireland*, HC 1849 (86),
xl, p. 123.
23 Letter of Sir Robert Gore Booth to
William Somerville, 4 Apr. 1848 (NAI,
CSORP 1848/z/3673); Copy of letter
from Sir Robert Gore Booth, 16 Mar.
1848 (PRONI, Lissadell papers,
D/4131/H/8); Swords, *In their own
words*, p. 303.
24 For the government's attitude see
Moran, *Sending out Ireland's poor*,
pp 70–90.
25 Richard Yeates to Henry Gore Booth,
27 Aug. 1847 in *Third report of the select
committee on colonization from Ireland*,
appendix, p. 124; see also Oliver
MacDonagh, 'Irish overseas emigration
during the Famine' in R. Dudley
Edwards and T. Desmond Williams,
(eds), *The Great Irish Famine: studies in
Irish history, 1845–52* (Dublin, 1956,
rep.), p. 338.
26 Fitzpatrick, 'Emigration, 1801–70', p. 593.
27 *Second report of the select committee on
colonization from Ireland*, pp 260–1,
p. 2651; p. 270, q. 2729.
28 Ibid., p. 275, q. 2787.
29 ibid., p. 275, q 2788–9; Coleman,
Passage to America, p. 202.
30 *Report of the state of the poor and on the
charitable institutions in some of the*

principal towns, with supplements contain-
ing answers and inquiries, poor inquiry
(Ireland), HC 1836, xxx, pp 60, 77.
31 Daniel J. Johnson, *Irish emigration to
New England through the port of St John,
New Brunswick, Canada, 1841 to 1849*
(St John, New Brunswick, 1996), p. 9;
*Copies or extracts of any dispatches relative
to emigration to British North America*,
HC 1851 (348), xl, p. 40.
32 See evidence of John Robert Godley
to Devon commission, printed in
*Appendix to minutes of evidence before the
select committee on colonization from
Ireland*, HC 1847–8 (737–ii), vi, p. 146;
SJ, 22 Dec. 1848.
33 Johnson, *Irish emigration to New
England*, pp 214–5.
34 *Second report of the select committee on
colonization from Ireland*, p.263, q. 2668;
Johnson, *Irish emigration to New
England*, pp 98–9.
35 David Hollett, *Passage to the new world:
packet ships and Irish Famine emigrants,
1845–1851* (Abergavaney, Gwent, 1995),
p. 122.
36 John Purden to Henry Gore Booth,
dated 17 Aug. 1847 in *Third report of the
select committee on colonization from
Ireland*, appendix x, pp 123–4.
37 Richard Yeates to Henry Gore Booth,
dated 27 Aug. 1847 in ibid, p. 124.
38 Patt and Catherine McGowan to their
brother Roger, dated 25 Dec. 1847 in
ibid, pp 125–6; MacKay, *Flight from
Famine*, pp 285–6.
39 H.M. Perley to John S. Saunders, dated
23 Feb. 1848 in *Papers relative to
emigration to the British provinces in
North America*, HC 1847–8 (932), xlvii,
pp 63–4.
40 Johnson, *Irish emigration to New
England*, p. 224.
41 M.H. Perley to John S. Saunders, dated
18 Sept. 1847; W.S. Harding to W.M.G.
Colebrooke, dated 13 Sept. 1847 in
*Papers relative to emigration to the British
provinces in North America*, HC 1847–8
(50), xlvii, pp 110, 128, 131–2;
Coleman, *Passage to America*, p. 201;
MacKay, *Flight from Famine*, p. 286.
42 W.S. Harding to the Mayor of St John,
dated 4 Nov. 1847, also J.R. Partelou in
Papers relative to emigration to the British

provinces in North America, HC 1847–8
(932), xlvii, pp 47–8.
43 Coleman, *Passage to America*, p. 200.
44 Moran, *Sending out Ireland's poor*,
pp 106–11.
45 Johnson, *Irish emigration to New
England*, pp 143–6; 143–6.
46 Peter Murphy, *Poor ignorant children:
Irish Famine orphans in St John, New
Brunswick* (Halifax, Nova Scotia, 1999),
p. 22.
47 Johnson, *Irish emigration to New
England*, pp 107–13.
48 See Power, 'Palmerston estate in
County Sligo', p. 130.
49 Murphy, *Poor ignorant children*, pp 5–7.
50 Copy of letter from Sir Robert Gore
Booth, dated 16 Mar. 1848 (PRONI,
Lissadell papers, D/4131/H/8).
51 Letter of B. Woolhoupter, dated 2 Sept.
1847 in *Papers relative to emigration to the
British provinces in North America*, HC
1847–8 (50), xlvii, pp 112–3; Johnson,
Irish emigration to New England, p. 215.
52 John Robertson to Henry Gore
Booth, dated 14 and 29 July 1847 in
*Third report of the select committee on
colonization from Ireland*, pp 122–3;
Coleman, *Passage to America*, p. 200
53 W.G.G. Colebrooke to Lord Grey,
dated 14 Dec. 1847 in *Papers relative to
emigration to the British provinces in
North America*, HC 1847–8 (932), xlvii,
p. 45.
54 Quoted in *SJ*, 15 Oct. 1847.
55 Adam Ferrie to Lord Grey, dated 1
Dec. 1847 in *Papers relative to emigration
to the British provinces in North America*,
HC 1847–8 (932), xlvii, pp 36–7.
56 M.H. Perley to John S. Saunders, dated
20 Jul. 1847 in *Papers relative to emigration
to the British provinces in North America*,
HC 1847–8 (50), xlvii, p. 90.
57 Extracts of resolutions proposed by the
Common Council of St John on 3
Sept. 1847 in *Papers relative to emigration
to the British provinces in North America*,
HC 1847–8 (50), xlvii, pp 111–2.
58 Ibid., 4 Nov. 1847 in ibid., p. 157.
59 Enclosure from T.F. Elliott to
B. Hawkes, 20 Nov. 1847 in ibid., p. 38.
60 Sir Robert Gore Booth to the
Colonial Office, April 1848 (NAI,
CSORP/z/36734).

61 An act to regulate vessels arriving from Europe with emigrant passengers, dated 30 Mar. 1848 in *Papers relative to emigration to the British provinces in North America*, HC 1847–8 (964), xlvii, pp 39–40; *Nation*, 26 Apr. 1848.

62 Bryan Clancy and his sister to his mother and brother, dated 17 Nov. in *Third report of the select committee on colonization from Ireland*, appendix x, pp 126–7.

63 Eliza Quin to her parents, 22 Jan. 1848 in ibid., appendix x, p. 128.

64 Catherine Bradley to her uncle, John, 6 Oct. 1847 in ibid., appendix x, p. 125; MacKay, *Flight from Famine*, p. 283.

65 *Third report of the select committee on colonization from Ireland*, pp 126–8.

66 Power, 'Palmerston estate in County Sligo', pp 131–2.

67 Mary Feeney to her father, 3 Aug. 1847 in *Third report of the select committee on colonization from Ireland*, appendix x, p. 131–2; John, Mary and Margaret Mullowney to their father, mother and brother, 4 Jul. 1847 in ibid., p. 127, *Second report of the select committee on colonization from Ireland*, p. 263, q. 2668, p. 264, q. 2671.

68 James M. Whalen, 'Almost as bad as Ireland': the experience of Irish famine emigrants in Canada, St John, 1847' in Robert O'Driscoll and Loran Reynolds (eds), *The untold story: the Irish in Canada* (Toronto, 1988), p. 163.

69 James Curred to his mother, 13 Dec. 1847 in *Third report of the select committee on colonization from Ireland*, p.129.

70 Eliza Quin to her parents, 22 Jan. 1848 and Mary McBride in ibid., pp 128, 131.

71 For an account of the background situation at Five Points see Tyler Anbinder, "'We will dirk every mother's son of you: Five Points and the Irish conquest of New York politics"; in *Éire/Ireland*, 36: 1–2 (2001), pp 29–31.

72 Marriage entries for 27 Feb and 26 Apr. 1854 (Marriage records for the Church of the Transfiguration, Five Points, New York, 1853–5).

73 See Tyler Anbinder, "'From famine to Five Points": Lord Lansdowne's Irish tenants encounter North America's most notorious slum', *American Historical Review* 107:2 (April 2002), pp 368–70; Anbinder, 'Palmerston and the Irish Famine emigration', pp 441–69.

74 Kerby A. Miller, *Emigrants and exiles, Ireland and the Irish exodus to North America* (Oxford, 1985), p. 293.

75 *Third report of the select committee on colonization from Ireland*, pp 127–8.

76 See Anbinder, 'Palmerston and Irish Famine emigration', pp 468–9; Moran, *Sending out Ireland's poor*, pp 119–20.

77 Copy of letter from Sir Robert Gore Booth, 16 Mar. 1848 (PRONI, Lissadell papers, D/4131/H/8).

78 McGowan (ed), *Constance Markievicz*, p. 57.

79 Coleman, *Passage to America*, p. 202.

80 Copy of letter from Sir Robert Gore Booth, 16 Mar. 1848 (PRONI, Lissadell papers, D/4131/H/8).

81 *Second report of the select committee on colonization from Ireland*, pp 266–7, qs 2692–3.

4. THE GORE BOOTH ESTATE AND POLITICS AFTER THE FAMINE

1 Vaughan, *Landlords and tenants*, pp 114–7.

2 Ryan, 'Lissadell estate of Sir Robert Gore Booth', pp 66–9.

3 W.E. Vaughan, 'An assessment of the economic performance of Irish landlords, 1851–81' in F.S.L. Lyons & R.A.J. Hawkins (eds), *Ireland under the union: varieties of tensions, essays in honour of T.W. Moody* (Oxford, 1980), pp 180, 187.

4 Dun, *Landlords and tenants*, pp 190–2.

5 *SC*, 27 Oct. 1851.

6 Vaughan, *Landlords and tenants*, pp 102–4.

7 See Gerard Moran, 'William Scully and Ballycohey – a fresh look' *Tipperary Historical Journal*, 4 (1992); pp 663–74; Dolan, *Earl of Leitrim*; Patrick Lavelle, *The Irish landlord since the revolution* (Dublin, 1870), pp 394–9.

8 Reply of Sir Robert Gore Booth to the address of the Ballymote tenants,

25 Jan. 1870 (PRONI, Lissadell papers, D/4131/Q1).

9 Address of Ballymote tenants, dated Dec. 1869 (ibid.).

10 Dun, *Landlords and tenants,* pp. 192–4.

11 Vaughan, Landlords and tenants, pp 122–3.

12 Vaughan, 'Assessment of economic performance of Irish landlords', pp 190–2.

13 Resolution of the Lissadell tenants, 7 May 1857 (PRONI, Lissadell papers, D/4131/H10).

14 Address of Ballymote and Lissadell tenants, 16 Dec. 1869 (PRONI, Lissadell papers, D/4131/H/9; D/4131/Q/1).

15 *SC,* 19 Nov. 1864.

16 Lewis, *Topographical dictionary of Ireland,* ii, pp 216, 513, 529.

17 Dun, *Landlords and tenants,* p. 190.

18 Ibid., p. 192.

19 James, *Gore Booths of Lissadell,* p. 57.

20 Death of Francis Goold (newspaper cutting, PRONI, Lissadell papers, D/4131/Q1).

21 *SC,* 19 Jun., 10 Jul. 31 Jul., 1847.

22 Ibid., 14 Apr. 1849.

23 Ibid., 9 Feb. 1850.

24 Quoted in *MT,* 13 Feb. 1850.

25 *SC,* 16 Feb.; 16 Mar. 1850.

26 Ibid., 20 Oct. 1851.

27 Ibid., 28 Apr. 1852; *Nation,* 11 May 1852.

28 *SC,* 22 Mar. 1852.

29 Ibid., 19 Jul. 1852.

30 Ibid., 31 Jan. 1852; James, *Gore Booths of Lissadell,* p. 46.

31 James, *Gore Booths of Lissadell,* p. 46.

32 *SC,* 31 Jan. 1852.

33 Ibid., 3 Nov. 1851.

34 Ibid., 3 May 1852; *Nation,* 18 May 1852.

35 *Nation,* 22 May; *SC,* 24 May, 28 Jun. 1852.

36 *SC,* 4 Oct. 1852.

37 Ibid., 15 Nov. 1852.

38 Hoppen. *Elections, politics and society in Ireland,* p. 125; Emmet Larkin, *The consolidation of the Roman Catholic Church in Ireland* (Chapel Hill & London, 1989), pp 354–5.

39 *SC,* 21 May 1859.

40 Ibid., 11 Apr. 1857.

41 Ibid., 11 & 18 Jan. 1868.

42 Ibid., 11 Jul. 1868.

43 Lord Palmerston to Sir Robert Gore Booth, 6 Apr. 1852; Lady Palmerston to Sir Robert, 13 Oct. & 29 Oct. 1868 (PRONI, Lissadell papers, D/4131/H/1).

44 *SC,* 23 Apr., 14 May 1859; 16 May 1868.

45 James, *Gore Booths of Lissadell,* p. 40.

46 *SC,* 29 Dec. 1876.